"One of the greatest needs of the church is the ability to [...] and failure from God's perspective. Steve Roy has provided much-needed help to equip Christians with the discernment to evaluate our lives and ministries with a biblical lens rather than a cultural one. Without trivializing sin, or minimizing the sting of failure, Steve helps us to see all of our lives through the redemptive power of the gospel."

Erik Thoennes, professor of biblical studies and theology, Talbot School of Theology, Biola University

"Bringing together deep pastoral and theological wisdom, Roy exposes the destructive power of the American narrative of success and failure, and points us to the pathway of grace and 'true success.' A must-read for all who are engaged in the ministry of the gospel!"

Peter T. Cha, associate professor of pastoral theology, Trinity Evangelical Divinity School

"Embedded in many cultures are the beliefs that we get what we deserve, and if we do the right things and try hard enough, we will not fail. Steve Roy provides a tender and hopeful countercultural reminder that for the Christian, God is the definer of our success and that Scripture is rife with human failings redeemed through grace. Roy persuades us to ask: How might we dare to love and serve others if we lived as beloved children of God, free from fear of failure?"

Susan Greener, associate professor of intercultural studies, Wheaton College

"For those on their way in their faith journey Steve's book is a succinct reminder and recitation of the limitless resources available to all of us as we cope with life's adversities. To those who have not yet begun their faith journey, it is a practical package of surprising support probably unknown to most."

Malcolm N. Briggs, CEO and chairman, Andesa Strategies, Inc.

"What does it mean to say that 'Steve Roy wrote the best book on failure'? Yet that is what I find myself saying and recommending to others. It's an excellent guide to failure. All of us know failure, but Roy's book

opens us up to a deeper understanding of how failure might be an important life-giving moment of new beginnings. It's in our failures that the good news is seen in all its flying colors."
Rev. Laura S. Truax, senior pastor, LaSalle Street Church

"I freely, though painfully, admit that fear of failure has shaped far too much of the way that I think and act. As a pastor, I also regularly counsel with folks staring what they perceive as failure in the face and being overcome by it. Personally and professionally, I consider Dr. Roy's insights a welcome gift that expose the core lies that too often shackle me and those I serve, and drive us back to the 'audience of one' whose view of us is the only one that truly matters."
Rev. Jeff Chadwick, senior pastor, First Presbyterian Church, Rome, Georgia

"Steven Roy's comprehensive identification and assessment of types, causes and results of failure paints a clear and accurate landscape of reality, in which we can find our own selves. The pastoral emphasis on God's grace in Jesus leads to the hope of real and lasting change as well as humble realism about ongoing failure and the need for continued grace."
Fred Bailey, Great Lakes East Regional Director, InterVarsity Christian Fellowship

"Steve knows failure, up close and very personal. Really hearing the words 'you are sicker than you think' changed his life. Rather than reacting with denial, silence or renewed attempts to make it, he responded with wisdom, seeking to understand how God defines failure and success and how he graces us to reach that goal. This is theology at its best. He grapples with success and failure biblically, discovering truths of grace. No one will work through this excellent study without being strengthened for struggles with inevitable failure in partnership with the Lord of compassion and grace."
Gerry Breshears, professor of theology, Western Seminary

STEVEN C. ROY

WHAT GOD THINKS
WHEN WE FAIL

Finding Grace and True Success

IVP Books
An imprint of InterVarsity Press
Downers Grove, Illinois

InterVarsity Press
P.O. Box 1400, Downers Grove, IL 60515-1426
World Wide Web: www.ivpress.com
E-mail: email@ivpress.com

InterVarsity Press® is the book-publishing division of InterVarsity Christian Fellowship/USA®, a movement of students and faculty active on campus at hundreds of universities, colleges and schools of nursing in the United States of America, and a member movement of the International Fellowship of Evangelical Students. For information about local and regional activities, write Public Relations Dept., InterVarsity Christian Fellowship/USA, 6400 Schroeder Rd., P.O. Box 7895, Madison, WI 53707-7895, or visit the IVCF website at <www.intervarsity.org>.

All Scripture quotations, unless otherwise indicated, are taken from the Holy Bible, Today's New International Version™ Copyright © 2001 by International Bible Society. All rights reserved.

While all stories in this book are true, some names and identifying information in this book have been changed to protect the privacy of the individuals involved.

Cover design: Cindy Kiple
Interior design: Beth Hagenburg
Image: Tortoise: Ivan Kmit/iStockphoto
 Boxturtle on its back: Steve McAlister/Getty Images

ISBN 978-0-8308-3939-1

Printed in the United States of America ∞

Library of Congress Cataloging-in-Publication Data

Roy, Steven C., 1954-
  What God thinks when we fail: finding grace and true success/
Steven C. Roy.
    p. cm.
  Includes bibliographical references and index.
  ISBN 978-0-8308-3939-1 (pbk.: alk. paper)
  1. Failure (Psychology)—Religious aspects—Christianity. 2.
Success—Religious aspects—Christianity. I. Title. II. Title:
Finding grace and true success.
  BT730.5.R69 2011
  248.4—dc23

2011023121

P	18	17	16	15	14	13	12	11	10	9	8	7	6	5	4	3	2	1
Y	26	25	24	23	22	21	20	19	18	17	16	15	14	13	12	11		

Contents

Preface

This book is a very personal one. It arose out of significant struggles with issues of success and failure in my prior ministry as a pastor. My experiences as a pastor and a professor have shown me that these issues are not unique to me or to those in vocational ministry. To one extent or another, every one of us has to face failure. So how should we gauge success and failure in our lives? What constitutes success? Who sets the standards and who evaluates how well or how poorly we have met them? And what do we do when we fail?

Note that I said "*when* we fail." Not "*if* we fail." The issue is not whether we will fail but how we will cope when we fail. Hence the title of this book: *What God Thinks When We Fail*.

I have sought to reflect the widespread experience of failure by incorporating stories of people from widely divergent groups and locations throughout the book. To all who had the courage to share their stories of failure and the lessons they have learned from their experiences, I say thank you; I owe you a deep debt of gratitude. I have tried very hard to express the gist of each of your stories faithfully and accurately, while changing appropriate details to make them anonymous. I realize that some of the stories have continued and progressed during the writing and editing of the book, but my commitment was to relay them as you told them to me.

My goal throughout this book is to explore how the vast resources of the Christian faith can enable us to cope wisely and well with experiences of failure. This book is intended to be an encouragement not only to my fellow Christ followers. It is also an invitation of hope to those who might be considering a relationship with Jesus Christ. To all, I invite you into the adventure of following Christ. His grace and truth will make all the difference when you experience failure.

A brief word about the structure of the book: After an initial chapter that shares some of my struggles with issues of success and failure, we turn to more general issues of success and failure. Because our experience of and struggles with failure can be understood only against the backdrop of success, we begin with a look at the nature of success—from the perspective of contemporary American culture (chapter two) and in the eyes of God (chapter three). We then turn our attention to the reality of failure (chapter four).

Then comes the heart of the book—a discussion of what I call "truths of grace," reflections on the theology in Scripture that can give us resources to cope wisely and well with failure in our lives (chapters five and six). Following that is a discussion of how we live out these truths as we respond to our failures (chapter seven). Chapter eight is a brief discussion of ways that those who are involved in ministries of various kinds can help others. It is written especially from the perspective of pastors and other church leaders (not surprising, considering my experience in pastoral ministry and my current role in training future pastors). But it also has application to other kinds of ministry and to other formal and informal opportunities to help others cope with failure. Finally, the epilogue reflects again on my own experiences with issues of failure and lessons I have learned.

I am grateful to the Board of Regents of Trinity International University for granting me a sabbatical in the fall of 2008, during which much of the work on this book was completed. Their generous sabbatical policy is a crucial way that the university supports research and writing on the part of its faculty.

I am also grateful to Gary Deddo and others at InterVarsity Press. Your editorial comments are always insightful and kindhearted. What a joy it is to work with you a second time!

Special thanks go to my wife, Susan Roy, and my daughter, Lydia McDermott, as well as to Peter Cha and Candy Poppino for reading all or part of this manuscript and offering substantial editorial assistance. This book is much improved because of your efforts.

Above all, I am thankful to my family for their support throughout the process of writing this book. To Andrew and Bethany, Beth and Dave, Lydia and Will: thank you so much. And supremely to Susan—my wife, my partner, my best friend and the one person who has taught me more about the reality of my own failure and the far greater reality of the grace of God than anyone else—to you I dedicate this book with all my love.

1

A Violinist and a Pastor

❦

A story is told of a young violinist who lived in London many years ago. He was a superb musician. He loved his music and enjoyed playing before small groups of people in the homes of friends. But he was deathly afraid of large crowds, so he avoided giving concerts. The thought of giving a public performance in a big concert hall absolutely terrified him.

The London music establishment was very critical of this young violinist. He was violating all the accepted protocols. According to the critics, excellent musicians were supposed to give public concerts in packed concert halls. In time, the criticism grew so intense that the young violinist relented; even though it scared him terribly, he agreed to give one major concert.

The largest concert hall in London was secured, and when the evening came, the hall was filled. People were excited to hear this prodigy. So were the critics, who filled the first three rows, pad and pen ready, eager to rake him over the coals.

The young violinist came onto the stage and sat alone on a stool. He put his violin under his chin and played for an hour and a half. No music in front of him, no orchestra behind him, no breaks—

just an hour and a half of absolutely beautiful violin music. After ten minutes or so, many critics put down their pads and listened, like the rest. They too were enraptured by the music of this young virtuoso. After the performance, the crowd rose to its feet and began applauding wildly—and they wouldn't stop.

But the young violinist didn't acknowledge the applause. He just peered out into the audience as if he were looking for something—or someone. Finally he found what he was looking for. Relief came over his face, and he began to acknowledge the cheers.

After the concert, the critics met the young violinist backstage. "It was just as everyone had anticipated," they said. "You were wonderful. But one question: Why did it take you so long to acknowledge the applause of the audience?"

The young violinist took a deep breath and answered, "You know I was really afraid of playing here. Yet this was something I knew I needed to do. Tonight, just before I came on stage, I received word that my master teacher was to be in the audience. Throughout the concert, I tried to look for him, but I could never find him. So after I finished playing, I started to look more intently. I was so eager to find my teacher that I couldn't even hear the applause. I just had to know what he thought of my playing. That was all that mattered. Finally, I found him high in the balcony. He was standing and applauding, with a big smile on his face. After seeing him, I was finally able to relax. I said to myself, 'If the master is pleased with what I have done, then everything else is okay.'"

As a follower of Jesus Christ, I resonate with this story deeply. Jesus is my Savior. By his death and resurrection, I have been reconciled to God and to his people. Jesus is my Lord, the only one who has the right to direct my life and to evaluate me in the end as to how well or how poorly I have lived my life.[1] And so I agree with the sentiment of the young violinist in the story: "If the master is pleased with what I have done, then everything else is okay." As a follower of Christ, I believe that, in the final analysis, his is the only evaluation that matters. If you are also followers of Christ, I hope you resonate with this as well. Believing this and seeking to live accordingly is a huge part of what it means to be a Christian.

When I'm honest with myself, however, I have to admit that it is much easier to say these things than to live by them. It's well and good to say that Christ's evaluation is the only one that really matters. But when I try to live that out, things start to get messy. Questions arise. How will Jesus Christ evaluate me? What are his standards? Perhaps more importantly, and certainly more difficult, how can I internalize his standards so that my own assessment of myself matches his? That's difficult enough in a vacuum. But when competing standards of success and failure scream at me from all sides, and when the evaluations of other people seem so much more tangible and immediate, it's hard to hold on to the conviction that God's evaluation of my life, my relationships, my work and my ministry is the only one that matters.

That's why I have written this book. I'm convinced that when we get these things wrong, it can be devastating. I know this from bitter and very painful experience in my former ministry as a pastor. Let me tell you a bit of my story.

A Painful Realization

My wife, Susan, and I were sitting in the office of a fellow pastor, Jack Harrison,[2] in the fall of 1992. The recommendation of friends had led us to Jack's office. "He's an amazing counselor," they said. That was what we needed, and our first visit confirmed that he was.

We had just spent the past hour pouring out our hearts about our lives and ministry at the church where I pastored. We had shared our doubts and questions, our discouragements and fears, the exhaustion and agony we were experiencing in our ministry. While there was a kind of cathartic release in telling the details of our story, we still needed insight into what was truly going on. And Jack, not one to mince words, said, "You're sicker than you think."

Those were hard words to hear, but they were filled with hope. A clear and accurate diagnosis was a necessary first step toward resolving the issues we were facing. "You're sicker than you think." How so? What was going on with us? Many components made up our crisis, but at the heart of it all was the issue of success and our perceived lack of it.

A little background is necessary to understand what had brought us to this point. I became a senior pastor for the first time in 1988. Prior to that, I had been an associate pastor of a large and growing church in the Midwest. But at the age of thirty-four I was called to the Pacific Northwest to become the senior pastor of a church that had been the flagship of its denomination in that region. Although the church had plateaued in recent years, its pastorate seemed like an impressive position for a young leader. However, as I came to work for this congregation, I was filled with the seeds of what would later bloom into a full-blown crisis regarding success—and failure.

Contributing Factors

In retrospect I can see several contributing factors that led to this crisis. Some were cultural. As an American, I had been born and raised in a culture enamored with success. This was the air I breathed. At their most basic level, typical American views of success involve what is *bigger* and *better*. Successful careers result in bigger salaries. Successful athletes are those whose statistics are better and whose teams win more games. Successful actors and actresses net bigger box office revenues than their rivals. Successful parents have children who get better grades in school and perform better than their peers in sports, music and drama.

"Bigger and better." That's success, American-style. However, since the "better" category is often hard to measure, there can be a strong temptation to determine success solely on the basis of what is bigger, which is measurable. For me as a pastor, whose vocation was inherently impossible to measure according to the "better" categories, measuring the success of my church in terms of the "bigger" categories was an attractive option.

The American culture not only gave me a vision of what success looked like, it also showed me how important success is. Americans love success and those who are successful. They hate failure; they fear it. Success is seen as the sure route to significance. Being successful ensures a healthy self-esteem and the approval of the most significant people in one's life. This is why the drive for success and the corresponding fear of failure are so strong. At the deep levels of my being, I had imbibed far more of these attitudes toward success and failure than I knew.

Not only had I been influenced by the broader American culture, I had also been shaped by the evangelical Christian subculture of the day. Among the elements of American evangelicalism in the late eighties and early nineties, the influence of the church-growth movement was very significant.[3] This movement began with a laudable effort to study growing churches and to learn common characteristics that mark these churches and their ministries. Church-growth principles were then developed so that other churches could shape their ministries in the same way. The best of these studies included both the "bigger" and the "better" elements of church life and ministry.

But, as with the broader culture, American evangelicals tended to minimize the "better" dimensions in favor of the more readily identifiable "bigger" dimensions.[4] Which are the "successful" (that is, growing) churches? Those with bigger congregations, larger budgets, more local staff, more missionaries, more conversions, baptisms, small groups, etc., etc., etc. In short, successful churches are the big ones.[5] Such was the view that had very subtly, but very powerfully, shaped me and the congregation I served. Deep down, we all knew that for this church—and this pastor—to be successful, the church would need to grow.

One other facet of church-growth thinking also influenced me. Of all the common denominators of successful, growing churches, the most significant was thought to be the pastor. Strong, visionary, charismatic pastoral leadership marked these growing churches. In fact, having such a pastor was considered the most crucial factor of all if a church was to grow.

At a theological level, I strongly disagreed with this conclusion. There is only one head of the church, and that is Jesus Christ himself (see, for example, Eph 1:22; 4:15; 5:23; Col 1:18; 2:19). He, not the pastor, is the most crucial person in the life and the growth of the church as a whole and of any particular local congregation. Note his unambiguous words: "On this rock *I* will build *my* church" (Mt 16:18, emphasis added).

But in spite of my theological convictions, the "facts" were there before me. Successful churches were led by a certain kind of pastor. And if I wanted to be successful, I needed to be this kind of pastor. The result? Intense pressure and very high expectations that I felt from both myself and the congregation.

Compounding this pressure was the complexity and difficulty of the role of pastor in the contemporary American church. Several generations ago, pastors were expected to preach and pray and visit the members of their congregations. Now a pastor is expected to do those things *and* be a visionary leader, a CEO of a volunteer organization, a spiritual director, a therapist, an evangelist, a motivational expert and a community leader. This intensified the pressure and stress I was experiencing. Though I felt called by God to this church, a gnawing question surfaced regularly: Did I have the gifts and abilities to do all that the pastoral role required of me?

Not all the influences that shaped me were cultural. I am also the product of my family of origin. I will be the first to say that I have been greatly blessed by God through my family. My parents and siblings are wonderful, and I wouldn't trade them for anything. But our family had always been a high-achieving one. Roys always did well academically and vocationally. The subtle yet very real message I absorbed growing up was that I needed to be successful to be significant. I had already taken a different path than others in my family in pursuing vocational ministry—a vocation that would never pay a lot. I reasoned that if I was going to be a pastor, I surely needed to be a successful one.

This is not an unrealistic expectation, I thought as I began my pastoral ministry in the Northwest. After all, my personal history had been filled with success. Growing up in this family of high achievers, I had followed suit. I did well academically at excellent schools for my bachelor's and M.Div. degrees. My prior ministry had been as an associate pastor of a congregation that fit the profile of a growing church. By the grace of God, it had been growing in all the "bigger" and "better" ways. It was fueled by a vision of a great and glorious God and by a philosophy of ministry growing out of that vision. And I was part of it! My ministry and my gifts had contributed, in some small way, to the growth of the church. Surely I was in a position to "spread the vision" in a new location.

My confidence only increased when I thought of the year our family had spent as short-term missionaries in Cameroon, West Africa. I had taught in a seminary there, and it had been a wonderful year. I had sensed the hand of God on me in teaching and preaching.

That was my background. And now I was coming to the Northwest as a senior pastor. I had the freshness and energy of youth, the gifts and calling of a pastor, and the "right" vision and theology. Not surprisingly, my hopes and dreams were high. Surely Susan and I were poised for success. Surely great things were in store for us.

All these factors combined to lead us to what I now realize were unrealistically high expectations as we entered this new ministry. When we came to the new church, we hoped that God would do the same kind of things there that we had seen him do in our former church. But not only did we hope for that, deep down we *expected* it.

The growth we desired God to bring in and through our ministry was inherently a good thing. We longed for a ministry that would honor God, build the church and impact the community and the world. No, the problem was not with the desires. The problem was that, without realizing it, our desires had hardened into expectations.

I have since come to believe that the difference between *desires* and *expectations* is a crucial one. It does not necessarily involve what we hope for. Rather, it involves the level of expectation we have—when our desire becomes a *demand* that what we hope for will come to pass. The difference between a desire and an expectation can be seen most clearly when the thing we hope for does not materialize. When a desire isn't fulfilled, we are disappointed. But when an expectation isn't met, we are *crushed*. We conclude that something is wrong. After all, we had not just wanted this to happen; we had not just hoped for it to happen; no, we had *expected* it to happen. It was *supposed* to be realized.

If you had talked to me in the summer of 1988, when I began my pastorate in the Northwest, I would have told you all the "right" things. I would have stressed that God is free and that he rarely does the same thing twice. I would have noted that our Northwest location was very different from our previous Midwest one. And the two churches were definitely different too. However, at a subconscious level, I was convinced that God would do the same kind of things—perhaps not to the same degree, but surely the same kind of things. After all, I was the new pastor. I shared the same theology as our previous church, the same vision of God, the same philosophy of ministry. And so the results would be the same. This was my expectation.

Our Experience at Church

As is the case with many ministries, we experienced an initial honeymoon period at the church. There was an air of excitement, good feelings on all sides and the anticipations of new beginnings. There was a season of slow but steady growth—numerically and in the far more important areas of worship, missions and theology. But almost three years into our ministry, I started to experience some significant criticism from various sectors of the congregation.

This is not at all uncommon in an older, plateaued congregation with a young pastor doing new things. But I will never forget one week in April 1991, when an elder unexpectedly told me he was resigning and leaving the church. At the top of his list of reasons for leaving was his dissatisfaction with my ministry as pastor. According to him, I was not similar enough in ministry style to my immediate predecessor.

I was completely caught off-guard. It was the first time in my adult life I had felt such a strong sense of failure and rejection, and it felt so personal. This elder and his wife were prominent, respected people in the congregation, and they were leaving the church primarily because of their dissatisfaction with me. What might that mean for the future? If a prominent elder was leaving, what would that say to the rest of the church? Was he right that I was the heart of the problem? The downward cycle of losing my confidence was beginning.

Later that very week, a second elder confronted me as he also resigned. According to him, my style and focus were not similar enough to the pastor who had served *before* my predecessor.

Stuart Briscoe once said that every pastor needs the mind of a scholar, the heart of a child and the hide of a rhinoceros.[6] Unfortunately I did not have such a thick hide. I was too young and too inexperienced to realize that much of the dissatisfaction had little to do with me. Other things were going on within the family system of the church—things that were present before my ministry began and that most likely remained after I left.

Over the next year and a half, the ministry of the church ebbed and flowed, but it never came close to matching my expectations. And the criticism never went away altogether. This made me very introspective about myself and my ministry. *Do I have what it takes to be a successful pastor? Should I stay here long-term? Would the church be better off with another pastor?* These were definitely not abstract questions. They were gut-wrenchingly personal. These questions about success and failure were not just about my ministry; they were about *me*. They filled me with doubts about my own gifts and abilities. They filled me with guilt. Had I worked hard enough; had I done enough? Were the problems at the church my fault?

I regularly struggled with fear about the future. After all, my ministry was not only my calling from God, it was also the way I provided for my family. If I decided to leave that position, how would I support my wife and three children? And this was my vocation, what I had been trained to do. Perhaps most significantly of all, these questions attacked my sense of identity. I was, after all, a pastor. So, what does it mean about me if I'm not a very good one?

Things came to a head in the fall of 1992, and as a result, we landed in Jack's office. We were physically exhausted, emotionally fragile and spiritually discouraged, with very little reserves and even less vision. We were filled with doubts and fears. It was not without reason that Jack said to us, "You're sicker than you think."

A Broader Problem

Such crises are certainly not limited to those in vocational ministry. Who among us has not faced issues of success and failure at work or in relationships? Is there not a crisis of success when a promotion at work that you wanted so much and thought you really deserved goes to someone else? Are not issues of success and failure right at the forefront when your sales manager is breathing down your neck, demanding an increased market share in your territory? Who among us would not struggle with a deep sense of failure when the family business that we are running is forced into bankruptcy or the family home goes into foreclosure? As a parent, is there not a sense of failure when your child's report card comes home with lower grades than you had hoped for, or when you get a phone call from the assistant principal telling you there has been a discipline problem at school and that your child is the main instigator? Would you not fear failure when your marriage is struggling and your spouse tells you that you're not meeting up to his or her expectations?

What We Needed

Jack challenged me and helped me to identify several things I needed to do to bring healing to our lives. He told me in no uncertain terms that I needed to "come clean" about my issues and struggles with the council of elders and with the congregation as a whole (not at all an easy task for a pastor who cared deeply what others thought of him and his ministry—but a necessary and ultimately very freeing one).

Susan and I also desperately needed to revamp our schedules to provide a healthier balance of work and family life and more sustainable levels of sleep and exercise. We needed some extended time away to give ourselves space to begin the process of healing. Most importantly, we needed to be reprogrammed by God. We needed new eyes to see the issues of success and failure from his perspective. We needed time, and we needed intentional effort to learn God's standards for success and to internalize them. The elders of our church granted us a leave of absence, and so began a process in our lives that continues to this day.

Jack recommended a book that quickly became a godsend to us: *Liberating Ministry from the Success Syndrome* by Kent and Barbara Hughes. God used this book greatly to help liberate me from false views of the nature of success. I have profited from the honesty of the Hugheses in telling the story of their struggles with issues of success in pastoral ministry. I also have gained a tremendous amount from the biblical insights that they share. And many of the thoughts I will offer in this book have been shaped and influenced by them.

Liberating Ministry from the Success Syndrome paints a clear and vivid picture of biblical success. And that's absolutely critical; we all need to learn God's standards of what constitutes success and failure. But there is a second component to most crises of success: learning how God would have us relate to success and to failure. We need to grapple with questions such as "Do I have to be successful to be significant?" "Is my identity necessarily tied to my success or my failure?" "What happens when I fail?" "How do I cope with failure?"

What God Thinks When We Fail is built on the conviction that all of us have two basic needs in this area: knowing what constitutes success and failure, and knowing how to respond to success and failure. It's crucial that we come to clear understandings of

God's standard of success. And we must realize that, even if we have the best and most accurate understanding of what it means to be a success in the eyes of God, all of us still fail at one time or another, in one way or another. We need to know how to cope with that failure as Christians.

But before we get to that, let's explore what God reveals about his understanding of success and failure.

2

In Whose Eyes?

CR

Thirty years ago, Tony Campolo wrote about the virtually irresistible lure of success: "Success is a shining city, a pot of gold at the end of the rainbow. We dream of it as children, we strive for it through our adult lives, and we suffer melancholy in old age if we have not reached it." In our culture, Campolo observed, failure is the "unforgivable sin."[1] It is to be avoided at all costs.

If this was true in American culture three decades ago, it is all the more true today. A Google search on the word *success* in early 2011 found more than 432 million results. Compare that to 284 million results in a Google search for *Jesus*. Contemporary Americans are obsessed with success. A recent search of the library database at Trinity International University, the school where I teach, produced 104 titles of books dealing with a broadly theological view of the issue of success. The same search, however, revealed only four titles of books on a theological understanding of failure. Failure, it seems, is not something we even want to think about.

But what is success? And how should we understand failure?

Preliminary Definitions
Merriam-Webster's online dictionary defines success as a "favor-

able or desired outcome." This is a relatively standard and not-at-all-surprising definition. But the definition continues: "the attainment of wealth, favor, or eminence."[2] Outcomes that would be considered favorable or desired will no doubt vary with the priorities and goals of the person involved. Cultural, socioeconomic, religious and generational factors, among others, are involved. But it is very revealing that Merriam-Webster's, a dictionary of American English in the first decade of the twenty-first century, specifies the kind of favorable outcomes that are most desired: "wealth, favor, or eminence."

It may be helpful for us to discuss success and accomplishment as they relate to these desired outcomes. One well-known success trainer, Doug Firebaugh, says that accomplishment occurs when a person engages in a task or action and obtains the desired results. But a single accomplishment does not necessarily constitute success. Success, according to Firebaugh, comes when one strings together a series of accomplishments that lead to a more significant life achievement. So he defines success as "an ongoing realization and obtainment of worthy desired results, concerning actions, life, business, wealth, or a worthy ideal."[3]

This is helpful in our understanding of success. A person does not become a successful chef by cooking one delicious meal. One is not a successful baseball player by hitting a home run in one at-bat. A single A on an exam does not make for a successful student. Accomplishment needs to be sustained before it results in real and significant "success." And conversely, one failure to accomplish an individual's goal does not establish her or him as a failure.

Significant in Firebaugh's definition of success is the need for the ongoing accomplishment of "*worthy* desired results." Not every set of regular and sustained accomplishments can truly constitute success. There must be the accomplishment of worthy goals. But that raises questions: What is a worthy goal? Who defines such a goal? Who evaluates my accomplishments and success? In whose eyes must I be a success in order to think of myself as successful?

The Significant Other

Why is it that some people feel very successful, even though the world in general may view them as failures, while other people have a deep sense of failure, even though the world may view them as very successful? Campolo suggests that the answer lies in an important truth: "We consider ourselves to be successful if the most significant people in our lives deem us successful."[4] We may call these very important people "significant others."[5] All of us have one or more significant others, and their view of us makes all the difference in whether or not we understand ourselves to be successful.

It is possible to be a prosperous and successful business executive or a talented and acclaimed artist, and yet to have never felt that you have measured up to the expectations of your parents. If they are significant others in your life, widespread recognition and applause from within the business or arts community will not mean nearly as much in terms of your own sense of self-fulfillment as the affirmation of your father and mother. For many of us, our parents, or others in our families of origin, remain very important significant others long after we have left that family unit. For others, it is a spouse or boyfriend or girlfriend who is that crucial significant other. For others, it is work associates and professional peers.

Significant others tend to change over the course of one's life. For young children, the key significant others are usually their mom and dad. If children know their parents are pleased with what they have done—whether it is the art project they've made in Sunday school, the way they say their lines in the school program, the grades that come home on report cards or how they perform on the soccer field—they almost burst with pride. Children feel love and approval when they feel they have measured up to what their mom and dad want. As a result, they view themselves as successful. As children grow, the time comes when their mom and dad lose their unique place as significant others. Who among us does not remember that transition from childhood to adolescence when the importance of our peer group started to overshadow our family in terms of our feelings of importance and success? What our mom and dad might think starts to fade in comparison to how our friends in school or the youth group at church feel about us.

Sometimes young people orient their behavior toward a general sense of what "everyone" is doing. They want to wear a certain style of clothes purchased from the right store, because that's what "everyone" does. Who is it that determines their taste in music, their social life on weekends, the values they hold to? Often it is the generalized "everyone."[6] Sometimes, a more specific and defined peer group rises in importance. That's where they want to fit in, where they want to be accepted. They find their sense of identity largely in terms of the group they are a part of, the group that accepts and approves of them. So they consider themselves to be one of the jocks, the nerds, the thespians, the preppies or the stoners.

As adolescence continues, attention and approval from the opposite sex becomes increasingly important. Most teens long for the admiration of that special girl or boy. Often adolescents do almost anything to gain the respect and value that comes from romantic attachments to members of the "right" group of guys or girls.

In adulthood, the composition of our significant others becomes more varied and complex. As we enter into significant romantic relationships (or long more deeply for them), these boyfriends/girlfriends/spouses become increasingly important significant others.

As we begin to form new families, the crucial impact of our families of origin rears its head again. It never really went away, even when its importance seemed to be eclipsed by our peer groups, but as we enter into adulthood, our families of origin once again become a dominant significant other in a whole host of conscious and subconscious ways.

As we progress in our education and enter into phases of training linked more closely to future jobs, the academic evaluations of teachers and mentors rise in importance in our minds and hearts. When we begin our careers, and certainly as we start to advance in them, the evaluations of employers, work associates and professional peers become very important. No less important are our customers, potential clients or the community we hope to influence.

If we are parents, we long for affirmation and approval of our parenting, from our own parents and from other parents we associate with. As our children grow, the sources of our affirmation as parents diversify. We derive great significance as parents from the academic, athletic, social and spiritual successes of our children. As they succeed, so we feel we do. In many ways, those who are significant others for our children become our own significant others. When our children become adults with their own families and careers, we often find the roles reversed and long for the approval of our adult children.[7]

Matt, a pastor friend of mine, confided that he very much longs to succeed in the public dimensions of his ministry. He longs for the worship services he plans and leads, the sermons he preaches and the leadership decisions he makes to be the best ones ever in the eyes of his congregation. He longs for the approval of those in leadership roles in the church, of his fellow pastors and professional peers, and of the community as a whole. This means he always has to be "on" when performing these public dimensions of his ministry. To be successful, he needs to perform well for these various public groups, for they constitute his significant others.

Mary grew up a little bit on the chubby side and was what she called "an early developer." This led to extreme self-consciousness, especially due to teasing in school. Her mom was strikingly beautiful (even the boys in her seventh-grade class commented on it) and was very concerned about weight issues herself. Mary's father was mostly absent, though he did encourage (or as it felt, pressure) her to get more exercise and more sun. The combination of lack of parental approval and her lack of acceptance by her peers led Mary to try a new approach to weight control and improving her appearance: purging what she ate through vomiting and laxatives. She was sure she could keep it under control, but in time her eating disorder started to control her.

Jennifer grew up in a family of high achievers, particularly in academics. When it was time for her to choose a college to attend, she followed the family pattern and picked a prestigious private college. But she was miserable during her first semester. She disliked most aspects of the school, and she missed her boyfriend, who was attending a state university. She saw a counselor to work through her feelings and decided to transfer to her boyfriend's school. But the very idea of transferring made her feel like a failure. "My family did not go to state schools, much less an average one, and *no one* followed their boyfriends/girlfriends anywhere. I was playing by completely different rules than the rest of my family. I felt like the odd one out, and I felt like a failure."

For many adults, the significant other is a more generalized group, often defined by one's social location. John is a retired physician who has had a long and successful medical practice. Yet he continues to feel a sense of shame because of a tendency he has to cry at moments of intense emotions. He feels his crying does not measure up to a cultural standard of masculine behavior. "Real men don't cry."

George is a former missionary who now runs his own company. Yet he regularly feels he does not measure up to his church's concept of "biblical manhood" or "leadership." As a result he feels like a failure. In comparison with the standards put forth by his pastor, he says, "I don't read and study the Bible enough, I don't memorize Scripture enough, I don't usher enough, I don't love and care for my wife enough, don't save enough, don't spend enough time with my neighbors, spend too much time at work, have a neverending list of home repair projects left undone, never am quite able to lose those last ten pounds, etc., etc., etc."

Sometimes our connection with significant others is more indirect. Early in my marriage to Susan, I regularly felt a nagging sense of failure because I was not particularly handy around the house, and especially not good at car repairs. I felt I didn't measure up to the example of Susan's father. He had passed away when she was in college before I met her, but I had heard enough from Susan to form an impression of her dad. And since I knew how important he was in Susan's life, my mental image of him became a significant other in my life. As it turned out, my picture of Susan's father was not entirely accurate. He was very helpful around the house and with neighbors, but he was not necessarily an expert at fixing the car. However, it took time before my emotions caught up with that reality and I was able to accept my mechanical limitations.

The point, I hope, is clear. It is those we consider to be significant others in our lives—whether they are specific individuals or broader and more generalized groups—who set the standards for us in our quest to be and to feel successful. Their evaluation is what matters most.

Success, American-Style

What constitutes success for us as Americans in the early years of the twenty-first century? While there is much variety in the specific standards of success held up by various segments of American culture, some generalized observations may be helpful.

In the previous chapter, I commented on the way many in our culture instinctively identify success with what is bigger and better. This is helpful, as far as it goes, but we need to ask, "Bigger and better with respect to what?" Let me suggest the following not-at-all-exhaustive list of areas in which our culture's "bigger and better" standard applies.

Wealth. Clearly wealth is prized in our culture. Our sense of status and place in the social order is often determined by the size of our salary. As my pastor has said, all too often our net worth defines our self-worth. Money makes some feel secure; it can enable others to feel powerful (if I control the money, I can make the decisions) and others to feel free to enjoy life.[8] Often this sense of freedom comes through the way we spend our money and the kind of material possessions we buy.

When success is measured by wealth, successful people are the ones who live in the "right" houses (often more than one), drive the "right" cars, wear the "right" clothes, travel to the "right" destinations on vacation, watch the "right" kind of televisions, utilize the "right" kind of technology and so on. In each case, the adjective *right* could be rendered "more expensive." We live in a consumer society, and lavish and conspicuous consumption is often seen as a highly desired outcome. The bumper sticker says it right for so many in our culture, "He who dies with the most toys wins!"

Our consumption is driven by the feeling of economic well-being, which for so long has been driven in the United States by gains in the stock market and housing values. Small wonder the recent economic crisis has hit so many so hard. Not only has it produced real economic hardship for many individuals and families, it has shaken the sense of economic well-being for many. If your view of success is tied to wealth, it's hard to feel successful when you watch your 401(k) drop by double digits.

The Christian community is not at all immune to the seductive influence of money and possessions. Church parking lots, especially in the suburbs, are filled with BMWs and Lexuses. Not only do Christians look to their comparative wealth and consumption to jockey for position and status with one another, a significant sector of the church views material prosperity as a sign of God's favor. This prosperity theology, which emphasizes God's commitment to provide abundant material possessions (along with professional success, and physical and emotional health) to all who have enough faith, arose in America around the turn of the century.

Prosperity theology is an important element of sectors within Pentecostalism (such as the Word of Faith movement connected to Kenneth Hagin, Kenneth Copeland and others), and it has been exported to many places in the developing world. A recent article in *Christianity Today* about prosperity theology in Africa suggested that adherents of this "prosperity-tinged Pentecostalism" make up more than a fourth of Nigeria's population, more than a third of South Africa's and up to 56 percent of Kenya's.[9] The prevalence of this massive (and, I'm convinced, misguided) movement points to the reality that among African Christians, as with their American counterparts, the link between wealth and success—even success with God—is very strong.

Prestige. We long to be recognized and applauded by others—the more the better. We want a high place in the pecking order of whatever group we are a part of, and we want our status to be clear and unmistakable to others. We want to have titles and degrees to print after our names. Getting the corner office is a sure sign that we have arrived.

Our culture is addicted to celebrity. The abundance of entertainment magazines and celebrity-oriented cable channels offers eloquent testimony to that. Paparazzi exist because of our insatiable cultural desire to witness the lives of the rich and the famous. Consider Andy Warhol's statement that everyone will be famous for fifteen minutes. More and more people seem to be craving fame; the proliferation of reality and talent-search TV shows points to this. At times we seek our own prestige through our connection with others who are famous. We want to make sure everyone knows that we know famous and important people—even if the term *know* stretches the truth to the breaking point. We engage in this kind of name dropping because we believe we can achieve status and prestige through the people we know. The acronym FOB (friend of Bill) used to be a badge of honor when Bill Clinton was president. Now it stands for "friend of Barack." Such is the lure of prestige as a criterion of success.

Power. The 2008 presidential election showed how much time, money and energy some are willing to expend to gain political power. The same could be said of myriads of candidates running for other federal, state, county and municipal offices. But it is not only political power that drives us. We long for economic power, for a larger market share, for a bigger role in the industry of which we are a part. We long for personal power. Office politics are often about who has power over what. Churches are wracked by petty squabbles over power and control, and over the way those with power exercise it. We think that if we have more power than someone else, we are more successful.

Beauty and youthfulness. Our culture highly values beauty, and beauty is regularly equated with youthfulness. The beauty of celebrities is highlighted in movies, on TV and in magazines. The standards of beauty portrayed surely are contributors to the high incidence of eating disorders. After all, if beauty is the ticket to success, we will do anything to get thin enough to be beautiful— even if that involves starving ourselves or engaging in other dangerous ways of losing weight. We spend hours working out at the gym, usually not to increase our overall fitness and health, but to lose weight or gain muscle so that we can look better. If we can lose the weight we want without having to work out, so much the better. So the weight-loss industry is thriving. In addition, Americans spend millions of dollars on beauty products, especially those that can help aging baby boomers retain the glow of youth. (Botox anyone?)

Sports. More and more of our young people participate in sports of one kind or another, and many parents encourage (or pressure) their children to participate at a young age. Many Olympic athletes tell of beginning their athletic careers very early. The drive to be successful requires more and more specialization at earlier and earlier ages. Youth league teams and traveling squads often dominate the lives not only of young athletes but also of parents.

From the very beginning, the crucial importance of winning is clear. (Sometimes it is more important to the parents of these young athletes than to the children themselves.) To be sure, trying one's hardest and competing fairly, according to the rules, are important. But as far as success is concerned, second place doesn't count. The oft-quoted mantra of legendary Green Bay Packers coach Vince Lombardi—"Winning isn't everything, it's the only thing"—carries the day in many sectors of our sporting culture.[10]

Sports are increasingly important not only for participants but also for fans. The rise of twenty-four-hour sports channels (how omnipresent ESPN is!) and fantasy football and baseball gives fans a virtual round-the-clock way to define their identity.

Competition. Our growing interest in sports reflects the crucial importance of competition in the way our culture views success of all kinds. Wealth, power and prestige are valued more when they are competitively gained than when they are inherited or simply have been handed to someone. We value those who work hard to achieve their success and who gain more of it than others. We admire those who have more money, more prestige, more power, more beauty or more athleticism than their peers.

Relationships and family. Many Americans define themselves in terms of romantic relationships, and ultimately in terms of marriage and children. No doubt, Americans today have more varied, flexible and individualized approaches to the timing of such relationships and how they are to be combined with careers than they did a generation ago. Yet when one's biological clock starts ticking loudly, the pressure to find the right relationship intensifies, as does the desire to have children. The rise in technologies and techniques for improving reproduction reflects not only incredible advances in medical knowledge and technology, but also the angst of those who are not "succeeding" in having children. When children do come and one becomes a parent, the anxiety over success does not end. To some extent every parent, and in our culture virtually every mother, defines success in life in terms of parenting. And with the inherent complexity and ambiguity of the task, a feeling of failure regularly rises to the surface.[11]

God as the Ultimate Significant Other

A central truth of the Christian faith is that God is the Creator of the heavens and the earth and all that is in them, including every human being who has ever lived. Since he is the Creator, he is the owner of all things and all people. And because he has created and owns all people, he will be their ultimate judge.[12] These foundational truths of Scripture are *objectively* true; final judgment by God through Christ will be the experience of every human being ("We must all appear before the judgment seat of Christ, that everyone may receive what is due them for the things done while in the body, whether good or bad," 2 Cor 5:10).[13]

However, living as a Christian involves more than a cognitive affirmation of these biblical truths. It involves a personal appropriation of them. This means, among other things, that we should consciously recognize God to be the ultimate significant other in our lives. We should invite him to play that role and continually seek to grow in valuing his perspective and his evaluation above all. To be sure, none of us does this perfectly. All of us are in process in this area. But as we seek to live faithfully as followers of Christ, we endeavor to look to his perspective above all.

This is not to say that the evaluations of others are insignificant or unimportant. But to live as a Christian means that we understand these human evaluations to be secondary. Our first and highest priority is to "do what pleases him" (1 Jn 3:22).[14] Jesus said in no uncertain terms that "no one can serve two masters" (Mt 6:24). His words force us to grapple with the practical impossibility of having multiple significant others operating at the same level of ultimacy. As a result, those who desire to follow Christ in this area must seek to grow in their ability to orient their lives around him and to seek his approval first and foremost.

As we do this, it is supremely important that we remember that this God, whom we follow as the ultimate significant other, is radically different from us and from the society around us. He says, " 'My thoughts are not your thoughts, neither are your ways my ways,' declares the LORD. 'As the heavens are higher than the earth, so are my ways higher than your ways and my thoughts than your thoughts' " (Is 55:8-9).

Overcoming by Being Overcome

There are few, if any, areas where this truth is more significant and more profound than in success and failure in life. A graphic example of this can be found in Genesis 32:22-32, where Jacob wrestled with God.[15] A little background can help us understand the import of this story.

Jacob and his twin, Esau, were born to Isaac and Rebekah. During Rebekah's pregnancy, God had declared to her, "Two nations are in your womb, and two peoples from within you will be separated. One people will be stronger than the other, and the older will serve the younger" (Gen 25:23). Before the twins were born, God chose the younger son, Jacob, over the elder son, Esau. As a result, Jacob would be the special recipient of God's covenant promises. He would be the one through whom God's covenant line would advance.

But throughout his life, Jacob could never fully trust God to bring this to pass. As he saw it, there were two major strikes against him: Esau was Isaac's eldest son, and as such he was entitled to the family birthright (a greater claim on the family inheritance and greater authority in the family hierarchy); and Esau was his father's favorite son, and therefore the most likely to receive Isaac's blessing. These obstacles seemed insurmountable to Jacob. So he decided that if he were ever going to receive those blessings, he would have to get them himself.

That was how Jacob lived. He spent over half of his life desperately (and most often deceitfully) trying to gain for himself what God had already promised to give him. Think, for example, of Jacob extracting from his famished brother the promise of his birthright in exchange for a bowl of lentil soup (Gen 25:29-34) and dressing up like Esau to deceive his aged father into giving him his final blessing (Gen 27:1-40). At one level, these deceptions "worked," and it seemed that Jacob had received much from his self-reliant scheming. But in the end, all he gained was what God had already promised him—that and his brother's enduring hatred. So he had to flee for his life.

At the end of his journey, Jacob met his match as far as trickery was concerned—his Uncle Laban. He was deceived by Laban into marrying his older daughter Leah instead of his younger daughter Rachel, whom he loved. Jacob had to work for Laban an additional seven years to marry Rachel (Gen 29:14-30). He vowed to get even, utilizing every trick in the book to multiply his own flocks of sheep, until he became so scared that he took his family and fled in the middle of the night, with Laban in hot pursuit (Gen 31:1-55).

In the end, Jacob did get what God had promised—for God always keeps his word. But throughout his struggle, Jacob tragically missed out on the peace and joy he might otherwise have enjoyed. By trusting in his own trickery instead of the promises of God, Jacob experienced years and years of anxiety and fear.

At no time, perhaps, was this fear more acute than the night he spent all alone beside the Jabbok River. Uncle Laban was behind him, but Jacob could only imagine an even greater danger ahead of him. He had received word that Esau was coming to meet him with four hundred men (Gen 32:6). For all Jacob knew, this was his brother's army out to take revenge on him after all these years.

Suddenly, out of the utter darkness of the desert night, a hand grabbed Jacob and "a man wrestled with him" (Gen 32:24). Imagine the terror. Was it an assassin sent by Esau? Was it a common desert bandit out to kill him for his clothes, sandals or staff? Whoever it was, Jacob was forced into hand-to-hand combat, struggling as if his very life depended on it.

The text indicates that this man who wrestled with Jacob was God himself, appearing in a human form (Gen 32:28, 30). But why? Why would God want to wrestle with Jacob?

I'm convinced it's because God wanted Jacob to trust him rather than his own ingenuity and resources. Jacob had lived his whole life based on the conviction that it was never safe to trust anyone else. You've got to take care of yourself; you've got to fight your own battles. And so Jacob fought on throughout the night. He struggled valiantly with all his strength until a crucial moment toward daybreak when he experienced a moment of excruciating pain. His hip had gone out of joint.

Can you imagine trying to wrestle with only one good leg? It's impossible. All you could do would be to cling to the other person for dear life. You'd hang onto your opponent with desperation—or you'd fall.

When God touched Jacob's hip so that it was wrenched, Jacob realized he could not support himself by his own strength. What a graphic way for God to show him what had been spiritually true of him all along! All Jacob could do was hang on.

When his opponent said, "Let me go, for it is daybreak," Jacob's response was immediate: "I will not let you go unless you bless me" (Gen 32:26). Somehow, through it all, he perceived that it was really God who was wrestling with him. And for once, Jacob's tenacity turned in the right direction. It turned toward dependence on God.

"I will not let you go unless you bless me." Those words of needy, dependent faith were what God had waited over forty years to hear from Jacob. Surely he would have preferred that Jacob recognize his dependence and cast himself on God's mercy long before this. But God loved him too much to leave him in the destructive rut of self-reliance. So he pursued Jacob in mercy and wrestled him into the submission of faith.

This change in Jacob was reflected by a new name that God gave to him. "Your name will no longer be Jacob, but Israel," God said, "because you have struggled with God and with human beings and have overcome" (Gen 32:28).

But how was it that Jacob had overcome in his struggles with God and with human beings? At the human level, Jacob had struggled his whole life, in many cases quite "successfully." But what had he really gained? He did gain, through his own resources, his brother's birthright, his father's blessings, his wives and his wealth. But none of these "victories" had brought him peace and joy and satisfaction. On the banks of the Jabbok, Jacob had struggled with God—and he had lost. God had touched his hip, and he was permanently wounded. Jacob was reduced to helpless dependence. And precisely in that dependence, Jacob overcame. When Jacob left that place, which he named "Peniel," for he "saw God face to face" (Gen 32:30), he left limping. He was weak, permanently disabled by God in his mercy. But as he limped off to meet Esau, he was stronger than he had ever been. He had overcome by being overcome. He had conquered by being conquered. He gained new strength by finally recognizing his weakness and by clinging to God in a tenaciously dependent faith. At last he was able to rejoice in the abundant blessing of God in his life.

Overcoming by being overcome. Such are the strange and merciful ways of God. Such are the upside-down values of his kingdom. How different than the insistent demand of Lombardi that winning is the only thing that matters in life. How different than our culture's insistence that a person has to win (in terms of wealth, power, prestige and so on) to truly be successful. Rather, this is like the paradoxical words of Jesus, "Whoever wants to save their life will lose it, but whoever loses their life for me and for the gospel will save it" (Mk 8:35).

My Ways Are Higher Than Your Ways

As we contemplate the standards of success put forward by our culture in light of God's words in Scripture, we are immediately struck by the fact that his ways are not like our ways and his thoughts are not like our thoughts. Indeed, the contrasts are overwhelming.

While our culture continually sets forth material wealth and possessions as the standard of success, Jesus has a different standard. He insists that people's lives do not consist in the abundance of their possessions (Lk 12:15). In one of his parables, Jesus identified as fools those who continually strive to accumulate more and more for themselves "but are not rich toward God" (Lk 12:16-21). Rather than obsessively trying to accumulate treasures on earth, "where moth and rust destroy, and where thieves break in and steal" (Mt 6:19) and where global economic crises can devastate their value, Jesus calls his followers to build up a far safer investment with a far greater return: treasures in heaven.

Followers of Jesus are called to seek first the kingdom of God and his righteousness, trusting that our heavenly Father will give us what we need (Mt 6:33). Armed with this conviction, we can be liberated from fear and greed and, as a result, experience the joy of contentment and generosity. Scripture reminds us that "godliness with contentment is great gain" (1 Tim 6:6) and that as we sell our possessions and give to the poor, we not only meet the needs of others but also provide for ourselves an indestructible treasure in heaven (Lk 12:33).

Our culture highly values prestige and the applause of others. But Jesus warns us against being like the Pharisees, for whom "everything they do is for people to see. . . . They love the place of honor at banquets and the most important seats in the synagogues; they love to be greeted with respect in the marketplaces and to have people call them 'Rabbi'" (Mt 23:5-7). For so many in our culture, such recognition would be a sure sign of success. But this is not the case in the kingdom of God. Jesus insisted, "The greatest among you will be your servant. For those who exalt themselves will be humbled, and those who humble themselves will be exalted" (Mt 23:11-12).[16] Oh, how strange and how wonderful are the upside-down values of the kingdom!

Surely the possession and the exercise of power is the mark of success, isn't it? But Jesus said that those who "lord it over" other people are actually abusing power. Instead, Jesus insisted that the pathway to true greatness is through being a servant (Mk 10:42-44). How different this is than competitive American views that see success as a win-lose game (if you win, I lose; but if I win, you lose).[17] By tying true greatness to being a servant, Jesus turned this on its head. True success, he said, is a win-win proposition. If others win, I win. This is the way of servanthood. This is the way of the kingdom.[18]

Rather than equating physical beauty with genuine success, God makes it clear that he does not evaluate people on the basis of their appearance. "The LORD does not look at the things human beings look at. People look at the outward appearance, but the LORD looks at the heart" (1 Sam 16:7). And Peter reminded women (and men) that their true beauty does not come from external adornment but rather from their inner self (1 Pet 3:3-4).

When it comes to standards of success, God's ways are not our ways. He is not at all impressed by all the things Americans are typically enamored with. This does not mean that his children should never pursue significant accomplishments in their careers or in their ministries. It is possible for Christians to use wealth and power wisely, to advance the ways of the kingdom. But it does mean that God never equates wealth, power, prestige or beauty with success.

If this is so, it raises another question. What *does* constitute success in the eyes of God?

3

Success in the Eyes of God

☏

The situation was desperate. The desert sun was hot. The ground was parched. The people and their livestock were suffering. And there was no water. It's hard to overstate the severity of this problem. Life in the desert without water is unlivable.

This incident in the history of the nation of Israel, recorded in Numbers 20:1-13, occurred forty years after God had delivered his people from slavery in Egypt. Confronting the absence of water, the Israelites did what God's people often do. They blamed their leaders: "Now there was no water for the community, and the people gathered in opposition to Moses and Aaron" (Num 20:2). Even after forty years of leadership, Moses and Aaron were still being attacked, opposed and blamed for the problems the people were experiencing. "They quarreled with Moses and said, 'If only we had died when our brothers fell dead before the LORD! Why did you bring the LORD's community into this wilderness, that we and our livestock should die here? Why did you bring us up out of Egypt to this terrible place? It has no grain or figs, grapevines or pomegranates. And there is no water to drink'" (Num 20:3-5).

Did you catch the pronouns the people used? "Why did *you*

bring the LORD's community into this wilderness . . . ? Why did *you* bring us out of Egypt to this terrible place?" Was Moses the one who had brought them out of Egypt? No! God was the one who had brought them out. Certainly he used Moses in the process. But there could be no doubt—God had been the ultimate deliverer of his people. Yet here in the parched desert of Kadesh Barnea, when times got tough, Moses and Aaron were held responsible. They became the target of the people's opposition.

Distraught because of the great need of the people and no doubt stung by the bitter accusations, Moses and Aaron responded in just the way we would want spiritual leaders to act. They went before the Lord, falling on their faces before him. God graciously appeared to them in his glory and gave Moses some very specific instructions: "Take the staff, and you and your brother Aaron gather the assembly together. Speak to that rock before their eyes, and it will pour out its water. You will bring water out of the rock for the community so that they and their livestock can drink" (Num 20:8).

Moses did just what the Lord instructed. Taking his staff with them, he and Aaron gathered the people together in front of the rock. But as he looked at those angry, ungrateful complainers, anger boiled up inside him. I think that forty years of frustration and opposition finally took its toll. He erupted, "Listen, you rebels, must we bring you water out of this rock?" (Num 20:10). He raised his arm and struck the rock with his staff. Not once, but twice. Water gushed out of the rock. And not just a little puddle. There was enough clear, cold water to satisfy the entire community and all their livestock.

What an incredible miracle! What a huge success for Moses! Just think what it must have meant for the members of the Israelite community. They had gone without water for so long. Their throats were parched. Their families were suffering. Their livestock were getting very weak, perhaps even approaching death. It is not surprising that they were angry. And now God had chosen to use Moses—the very one they had blamed for their situation, the object of all their scorn and hostility and opposition—to meet their needs in such a mighty way. I have no doubt that after water gushed from the rock, Moses was regarded as the hero of his people. As it was in the exodus, so once again, Moses was the great deliverer. I imagine that the people gave glory to God and applauded Moses. It was another resounding success in Moses' life.

However, in the eyes of God, things were very different. Moses had not succeeded at all. In fact, this very occasion that the people had no doubt regarded as one of Moses' greatest successes was actually his greatest failure. God had very explicitly told him to *speak* to the rock. But in his anger and lack of faith, Moses disregarded God's command and struck the rock, not once but twice.

In God's eyes, Moses' failure was of such massive proportions that the consequences were severe. In Numbers 20:12, the Lord said to Moses and Aaron, "Because you did not trust me enough to honor me as holy in the sight of the Israelites, you will not bring this community into the land I give them." Because they did not trust God enough to obey his explicit commands, Moses and Aaron would never be able to fulfill their cherished dreams of leading Israel into the Promised Land.

"Success" Is in the Eye of the Beholder

When we look at this incident, there is an important lesson for us to learn. It is possible to be regarded as hugely successful in the eyes of the world, yet not at all be successful in the eyes of God. You and I can give other people exactly what they need. We can have the approval and applause of all our significant others. We can be appreciated and admired by our peers, our family and friends, our boss and coworkers, our neighbors and even ourselves, but not be a success in the eyes of God. It doesn't matter how many promotions we might be given at work, how much our salary might rise, how much prestige we might enjoy in the eyes of the community; if we're not faithful to God, we're not success-ful. And conversely, if we are genuinely faithful to God, trusting him enough to be obedient to him, we are truly successful, no matter what anyone else might say about us.

Jesus told a parable about a man who was hugely successful by the standards of material wealth (Lk 12:16-21). His harvests were so abundant that he had to build new barns to store all his crops. Surely this was more than enough to provide for him and to enable him to "take life easy; eat, drink and be merry" (Lk 12:19). He was a great success. Everyone could see it. But that was not God's per-spective. In his eyes, this man was a "fool," for while he was busy storing up things for himself, he was not "rich toward God" (Lk 12:20-21). Though this man was very successful by human standards of wealth and prosperity, in the eyes of God he was a tragic failure.

Contrast this with the experience of John the Baptist. He took a courageous stand for righteousness in confronting Herod about his unlawful marriage to Herodias, and he ended up being be-headed for it (Mt 14:1-12). This does not at all seem to be a sign of a "successful" ministry. Yet Jesus commended him in glowing terms: "I tell you, among those born of women there is no one greater than John" (Lk 7:28).

Success in the eyes of other people and success in the eyes of God are not necessarily the same things. It is very possible to have one but not the other.

What God Is Looking For

Numbers 20 is clear. God is looking for faith. He wants his people to trust him. Faith is what we need to honor and please God: "Without faith it is impossible to please God" (Heb 11:6). But God is not just looking for professions of faith. No, he wants his people to trust him enough to obey his word.

The connection between faith and obedience can be illustrated by looking at the relationship of a doctor and her patient.[1] Imagine yourself to be very, very sick. You go to the doctor, and she examines you. After the examination, your doctor says that she has both good news and bad news for you. The bad news is that you are very sick, dangerously so. But the good news is that she knows what will heal you, and she proceeds to write a prescription for medication to take.

At this point, the question becomes, if you really trust your doctor, what will you do with her prescription? The answer is obvious: you will take the medicine. If you don't, your actions say loud and clear that you don't really trust your doctor. Perhaps you think she is not competent or that you know better than she does what will make you well. But, for whatever reason, your unwillingness to follow your doctor's orders says volumes about your lack of trust.

So it is with our relationship to Jesus Christ. He comes to us and tells us in no uncertain terms that we are sick—sick in rebellion, sin and brokenness. But in mercy and grace, he tells us what will make us well. He calls us to follow him.[2] That's his prescription for us. So the question is, if we really do trust Jesus, what will we do in response to his call? We will accept it, we will embrace it, and we will become his followers.

As we seek to follow Jesus, we regularly find ourselves facing choices in which we must decide whether to obey him or not. Every one of those decisions is fundamentally an issue of faith. For example, when we hear Jesus say to us that loving and forgiving our enemies is a more joyful and God-honoring way to live than holding onto grudges and seeking revenge (see Mt 5:43-48; 18:21-35), we must decide. Whom will we trust? Will we trust Jesus enough to follow his way of forgiveness and love? Or will we trust the voices of the world around us and of our own fallenness that assure us it's only natural to refuse to forgive those who hurt us and that revenge is truly the sweetest of victories?

When Jesus tells us that our lives do not consist in the abundance of our material possessions and that we should instead be characterized by generosity and contentment (Lk 12:15; 2 Cor 9:5-13; Heb 13:5), will we trust him enough to order our lives in this way? Or will we end up trusting the promises of our consumer culture and find ourselves serving money rather than God? When Jesus calls us to fidelity and permanence in marriage (Mt 19:1-12), will we trust him enough to follow him in obedience, or will we trust the siren song that says if I only had another partner I would really be happy? The list could go on and on, but I hope the point is clear. The fundamental issue in following Jesus is one of faith. If we trust him, our faith will inevitably lead us to follow his prescription for our lives.

So it is not surprising that in his devastating critique of Moses and Aaron, God zeroed in on the issue of faith—a faith that trusts God enough to be obedient to him. "Because you did not trust in me enough to honor me as holy in the sight of the Israelites, you will not bring this community into the land I give them" (Num 20:12).[3] Faith in God that leads to obedience is regularly identified in Scripture as the key to success in the eyes of God.

Why Strike the Rock?

One more point about Numbers 20 before we leave this text. Why did Moses strike the rock? He was a man of faith, whose whole life had been characterized by trust in God (see, for example, the description of Moses in Heb 11:24-29). So why did he fall into unbelief and disobedience here? Why did he strike the rock when God explicitly told him to speak to it? Let me suggest an answer: it had worked before.

Almost forty years earlier, Moses had confronted a similar situation—parched and angry people in the desert with no water (Ex 17:1-7). At that time, God told Moses to take his staff and strike the rock so water might come out of it for the people to drink. Moses did this, and God fulfilled his promise. He brought water out of the rock.

Here in Numbers 20, in a very similar situation, with Moses feeling the pressure to meet the needs of the people, the overwhelming temptation was to go back to what had worked in the past. That's a temptation we all can feel. In the midst of a crisis of success, of feeling the overwhelming need to be successful and fearing that we aren't, the pressure can become very great to disregard God and go directly to what has worked for us in the past. Or we feel the pressure to go to what has worked for someone else—for friends and family members, for the coworker who seems to be more successful than we are, for other people who have great marriages or who seem to be raising wonderful children, for the pastor of the "successful" church down the street. We read self-help books and advice columns. If only we can do what other successful people have done, we can be just as successful as they are. Or so we think.

Faith and Faithfulness

Another word for the obedient faith that God is looking for is *faithfulness*.[4] This is what Jesus highlighted in his parable of the talents (Mt 25:14-30). As a master was leaving on a long journey, he entrusted his wealth to his servants, commanding them to put it to work while he was gone. Two of the servants did what their master had commanded, and they were praised for their faithfulness. "Well done, good and faithful servant!" (Mt 25:21, 23). A third servant, however, was so afraid of failure that he was unwilling to take any risks at all. He didn't trust the goodness and fairness of his master, so he buried the master's money in the ground. In the end, he was severely rebuked.[5]

Jesus said he will reward faithful servants. Those who are willing to invest the gifts, talents, abilities, time and energy they have received from the Master to follow him faithfully will live under the smile of God here and now. This is true no matter how much money they make, no matter how much prestige and approval they enjoy in the eyes of others, no matter how much power they possess. And it is these servants, who faithfully follow God in whatever he calls them to do, who will hear his words of commendation and praise on the last day. They are the ones who will share in their Master's happiness throughout eternity (Mt 25:21, 23).

Where might we find this kind of faithfulness? It can evidence itself, for example, in a marriage. My parents celebrated their sixtieth wedding anniversary last summer. While they would be the first to admit that their marriage is not perfect and that it hasn't always been easy, I admire their love for one another and their desire to serve each other—all the more as they have gotten older and have to deal with various physical limitations. Their committed faithfulness to one another—not just in remaining married but also in honoring and cherishing each other above themselves for sixty years—makes them great in the eyes of God.

Persistent, loving faithfulness is a hallmark of many parents. A friend of my wife has tirelessly given herself to the care of her daughter who has severe developmental disabilities. She has lovingly cared for her from birth to adulthood. Again and again she has put her daughter's needs above her own. It is not necessarily the kind of life that achieves celebrity status in magazines, blogs and television shows. But it is the kind of faithfulness that is precious to God and surely makes her successful in his eyes.

Jesus highlighted the faithfulness of a poor widow who placed two very small coins into the temple treasury (Lk 21:1-4). Though it was all she had, she was faithful to God in her giving to support the ministry of the temple. Though the amount she gave was small, her faithfulness was great.[6]

Jesus commended giving and other spiritual practices such as fasting and prayer when they are done quietly (Mt 6:1-18). While the public applause from such quiet acts of faithfulness will be small to nonexistent, our heavenly Father "sees what is done in secret" (Mt 6:4, 6, 18), and he rewards faithfulness.

It is confidence in the reward of our heavenly Father that can motivate us and sustain us in ongoing efforts to love and serve the poor, the disabled, the disenfranchised and all others who can never "pay us back."[7] Jesus said,

> When you give a luncheon or dinner, do not invite your friends, your brothers or sisters, your relatives, or your rich neighbors; if you do, they may invite you back and so you will be repaid. But when you give a banquet, invite the poor, the crippled, the lame, the blind, and you will be blessed. Although they cannot repay you, you will be repaid at the resurrection of the righteous. (Lk 14:12-14)

All of these are pictures of the faithfulness God desires and that constitutes success in his eyes. This is why Mother Teresa said, "I do not pray for success [in the eyes of the world], I ask for faithfulness."

Good News About Success

This biblical teaching about success in the eyes of God is very good news for us.

At first glance, this may seem like a strange statement. After all, faithfulness to God is an incredibly challenging criterion of success. It probes deeply into our hearts. Our culture may content itself in defining success in terms of external things—money and possessions, status and popularity, power and influence, appearance and beauty—but Jesus defined success in terms of the heart.[8] So how is this good news? After all, who among us is always faithful to God? Have we not all failed again and again to express that faithfulness by humbling ourselves to love and serve others?

It is certainly true that all of us have failed—and will continue to fail—to meet this standard. Scripture is filled with good news about the ways that the grace of God meets us in our failure. That's the burden of the remaining chapters of this book. But at this point, I want to mention another reason why this biblical understanding of success constitutes good news. This understanding means that genuine success is available to all of God's children.

Few of us will be hugely successful in the eyes of the world. Not many of us will climb to the pinnacle of the corporate ladder or become all-star athletes or Oscar-winning actors or actresses. The vast majority of us just don't have the rare combination of gifts and abilities to excel above our peers. As a result, we will never be famous and receive the widespread acclaim and applause we so often link with success. If we are limited to these cultural understandings of success, most of us can never hope to be successful.

But all of us, as followers of Christ, can be faithful to God. Faithfulness does not require extraordinary gifts or a large stage or public notoriety. It's not dependent on having a certain amount of money or education. It's not dependent on good luck or fortuitous circumstances or knowing the right people. Every one of us can love God. Every one of us can be a loving servant to our neighbors. We can all humble ourselves. You and I don't need to be in good health to love God. We are never too young or too old to love our neighbor. We can all be servants, whether we are married or single, employed or unemployed, illiterate or holding a Ph.D.

The fact that none of us will ever do all this perfectly this side of heaven does not change the fact that significant progress is possible.[9] If we humble ourselves to receive God's love, and if we trust him to change our hearts and empower us to live a life of humble, loving faithfulness, every one of us can be truly successful in our lives. And that is good news!

Adding to this good news is the fact that our ultimate significant other is the all-seeing, all-knowing God. The one who will be our judge is omniscient. No act of faithfulness on our part, no matter how small, no matter how unappreciated in the eyes of others, will ever go unnoticed by God. He knows, and he will reward his faithful people. "Well done, good and faithful servant!"

The Crucial Issue of Timing

The question of *how* God judges and evaluates genuine success is absolutely critical. But every bit as important is the issue of *when* God makes this evaluation and when we should as well.

The apostle Paul wrote about both of these issues.

This, then, is how you ought to regard us: as servants of Christ and as those entrusted with the mysteries God has revealed. Now it is required that those who have been given a trust must prove faithful. I care very little if I am judged by you or by any human court; indeed, I do not even judge myself. My conscience is clear, but that does not make me innocent. It is the Lord who judges me. Therefore judge nothing before the appointed time; wait till the Lord comes. He will bring to light what is hidden in darkness and will expose the motives of people's hearts. At that time, each will receive their praise from God. (1 Cor 4:1-5)

Paul was very clear as to what God required of him in his ministry. It was faithfulness. As one entrusted with the mysteries God had revealed, Paul was a steward, obligated to act faithfully, in accordance with the goals and desires of his Master. Only by such faithfulness would he ultimately be found to be successful in the eyes of his Lord. And this would be true no matter what the human response might be to his ministry.[10]

So focused was Paul on the Lord as his ultimate significant other ("It is the Lord who judges me") that he was able to keep the evaluations of others in perspective. No doubt, the Corinthian believers had their opinions about him. They made their judgments (just as all of us make evaluations and judgments about church leaders, political candidates, entertainers and public figures of all kinds). But their evaluations, no matter how positive or negative, were not a big issue for Paul. He was so intent on being faithful to God in his life and ministry that he could say, "I care very little if I am judged by you or by any human court."

Paul didn't even spend much time judging himself. He recognized he didn't know all the recesses of his heart. He understood that only God can judge perfectly. So Paul sought to live in such a way that his conscience was clear, and he was willing to wait for God to pass his judgment, which he will do on the last day when Christ comes again. Paul's words to the Corinthians are filled with wisdom for all of us: "Judge nothing until the appointed time; wait till the Lord comes."

We must remember that any evaluations that are made now are not final. Any judgments of our success or lack of it—whether they are the judgments of other people or of us—are only provisional. They are like the score of a baseball game at the end of the fifth inning. Knowing whether a team is ahead or behind can help a manager come up with wise strategies for how to play the rest of the game. But no baseball manager, player or fan mistakes the score in the fifth inning for the final score of the game. There is more of the game to be played. And sometimes the final score can be very different from what was expected mid-game.

As a fan of the Chicago Cubs, I learned this truth the hard way.

The Cubs were five outs away from going to the World Series in the 2003 National League Championship Series. They had a three-games-to-two lead over the Florida Marlins, and they were leading 3-0 with one out in the eighth inning when a fan named Steve Bartman interfered with a foul ball down the left field line. With new life, the Marlins rallied to win game six and then game seven, and eventually the World Series. The Cubs lost; the Marlins won. As Yogi Berra famously said, "It ain't over till it's over."

We need to remember this.[11] Through our faithfulness to God, we can sense his pleasure with us now. We can rejoice in his love and be filled with hope at his ultimate words of praise and commendation, "Well done, good and faithful servant!" But Scripture would always have us remember that the final score is not in. Success at any point in our lives does not, in and of itself, guarantee future and final success. And present failure does not doom us for the future. This is the way of wisdom. "Judge nothing until the appointed time; wait till the Lord comes" (1 Cor 4:5).

Responding to Success

If, by God's grace, we are successful, what should our response be? How should we react if we achieve the kind of success that is noticeable and apparent to others? Far more importantly, how should we respond to the deep faithfulness of God that constitutes true success in his eyes? Let me suggest two God-honoring ways.

First, we must be grateful to God. The apostle Paul asked a very penetrating question to the church in Corinth, a church that had been so richly blessed by Christ in every way: "What do you have that you did not receive?" (1 Cor 4:7). The answer, of course, is "nothing!" Everything we have comes to us from God. He is the one who "gives everyone life and breath and everything else" (Acts 17:25). And this includes our success. All success ultimately comes to us from God. All of it is a gift of grace. Paul went on: "What do you have that you did not receive? And if you did receive it, why do you boast as though you did not?" The grace of God is never earned or deserved by us; it is always a free gift. So it should humble us. And it should make us very grateful, grateful to God who is the giver of all true success as he is of every other good gift.

There is something lurking deep within our fallen nature that loves to take credit for the success we experience. As a result, those who achieve academic success may be tempted to boast in their intelligence and hard work. Those who rise to the top in the business world may love to credit their success to their own intelligence, strategies and work ethic. Artists may boast of their creativity and skill. Parents whose children are living good lives can be tempted to credit it to their child-rearing philosophies, their communication abilities or their emotional availability. And those who deep down feel that they are so very "blessed" often don't direct their thanksgiving in any particular direction. The amorphous feeling of "being blessed" seems to be enough.

But children of God know who the source of all their blessings is. It is their heavenly Father. Even the faith that enables them to love and to serve is a gift from his grace. Paul wrote, "For it is by grace you have been saved, through faith—and this is not from yourselves, it is the gift of God—not by works, so that no one can boast" (Eph 2:8-9). The faith that saves us, initially and throughout a lifetime of good works (Eph 2:10), is a gift from God.[12] So we dare not boast in ourselves.

In light of this, perhaps we should add gratitude to our list of qualities of heart and life that constitute success in the eyes of God. It's hard to imagine how an ungrateful, bitter, complaining, self-exalting Christian could be successful in the eyes of God. Being thankful is at the heart of how we can "worship God acceptably with reverence and awe" (Heb 12:28). And nothing could be more important than that.

If we are successful—in the eyes of the world, and far more importantly in the eyes of God—our success is a gift of God's grace. And in response, we must be humble and thankful.

Second, it is important for us to respond to our success with new resolve for ongoing faith and obedience. Since the final score of our lives is not in, we cannot rest complacently on our prior success. We all know, from Scripture and from experience, of far too many cases in which people make impressive beginnings only to end poorly.

From Scripture, we learn of Solomon, who ruled as king of Israel with unparalleled wisdom and grace. He built the temple in Jerusalem. Yet in the end, his wives turned his heart toward other gods. He did not remain faithful to Yahweh and experienced his anger and wrath (1 Kings 11:1-13). Success in one area of life (ruling as king) doesn't prevent failure in other areas of life.

We think of the institution of marriage in the United States in the twenty-first century. Statistics tell us that close to half of American marriages will end in divorce.[13] But no one begins a marriage planning on divorce. Most begin their marriages filled with hopes and dreams for ongoing love and joy. They begin well, but they don't end well. This is not meant to suggest that all marriage partners share equal responsibility for a divorce or that every decision to divorce is necessarily a wrong one. All I am saying is that marriages that end in divorce do not fulfill the initial hopes and dreams for the relationship.

Though it is all too possible to begin well and yet to end poorly, the reverse is also true. Those who begin poorly can, by God's grace, finish with amazing success. Saul of Tarsus was a persecutor of the church. But Jesus appeared to him on the Damascus road and called him to be his witness to the Gentiles. By God's grace and through repentance and faith, Saul the persecutor was transformed into Paul the apostle.

Abraham Lincoln's early days in politics were anything but successful. He lost elections for the Illinois House of Representatives, the U.S. House of Representatives and the U.S. Senate before being elected president of the United States in 1860 and going on to be arguably the greatest president in American history.[14]

When we find ourselves being successful, how should we respond? By God's grace, let us do so with humble gratitude and with fresh resolve to be faithful to God in all areas of our lives.

4

Experiencing Failure

☞

We turn our attention now to the primary topic of this book: failure and the ways our Christian faith can help us cope with it. We have spent considerable time looking at the flipside of this issue, looking at success and how it is determined by our culture and by significant others. Far more importantly, we have looked at success as God evaluates it. This has been a necessary part of our study. But many of us stop here. We would much rather think about success than about failure. In American culture, success is revered, and failure is ignored, denied and denigrated. Failure, we think, must be quickly overcome and eliminated.[1] But we all fail, in one way or another and at one time or another. The question is, what should we do *when* we fail?

What Does Failure Look Like?

Failure comes in all shapes and sizes. Just as success involves meeting the standards set by our culture, by significant others and/or by God, so failure involves *not* meeting those standards. We may perceive failure in terms of wealth, power, prestige or any other socially defined measure of success. Our failures may be relatively small, or they may be huge and life altering. Our experience of failure may be a faltering business, an unsuccessful job search, a criminal act or a destructive behavior prompted by an addiction. We may experience as failure the absence of a desired relationship or problems in relationships that do exist. We may find ourselves wistfully looking at opportunities we've not pursued, or we may be filled with regret over a lack of accomplishment in directions undertaken. Or, in deeper and ultimately far more important ways for us as Christians, we may realize that we have failed God. We have not been faithful to him, we have not loved him and our neighbors as we should, and we have failed to humble ourselves and be grateful to him.

Failure in this sense can be understood objectively—actual failure in the eyes of God. And as we will see, it is very important for us to be able to assess our lives and discern where we have actually failed God. This is what opens the door to repentance and to the gift of forgiveness. But failure is not only something we assess. It is also something we experience subjectively—often with agonizing intensity.

It is here, in the area of subjective experience, that much of the variation in our response to failure occurs. How we perceive our failures is a crucial factor in how we feel about them. But there seem to be several factors that determine the intensity of our feelings of failure.

We can experience failure both in the small areas of our lives and in larger and more important ways. Our failures can be occasional and infrequent, or they can be regular and habitual. We can experience notorious failures that result in public shame or private failures that are known only to ourselves and perhaps to those closest to us. The intensity of our feelings of failure can vary depending on each of these. To the extent that public audiences of our failure are our crucial significant others, we may feel our failures more acutely. The larger and more frequent our failures are, the more we will be tempted to form our identity from them. When our experiences of failure seem to us to be large and habitual, we may start to view *ourselves* as failures.

Another factor in our subjective response to failure is *guilt*. Sometimes we are genuinely at fault—legally and/or morally. In those cases, we are culpable for our failures. We feel guilty about them because we really *are* guilty. But on other occasions, what we experience as failure is actually the fault of someone else. Living in a fallen world, we both sin and are sinned against. This crucial relationship among failure, sin and guilt will be explored more fully in the next chapter, but for now, it is important to recognize that our feelings of failure are exacerbated when we believe we are at fault. Whether we really are guilty or not, our subjective, emotional sense of failure is intensified when we *think* we are.

Closely related, though not identical, with the issue of guilt is that of *responsibility*. Even if we are not morally blameworthy for our inability to accomplish a goal or to meet a standard, we may still feel responsible. If it is our action or inaction that has resulted in the failure, we sense that the responsibility is ours. Even if the decision we made was the wisest one we could have possibly made at that time, knowing what we knew at that time, we still bear a sense of responsibility. And our feelings of failure likely grow stronger as a result.

Another factor that can intensify our feelings of failure is the knowledge that our failures *impact other people*. At times the numbers affected are large; other times the impact of our failure is restricted to just one person.

All of these dimensions are significant in determining the intensity of our feelings of failure. All increase our sense that at some basic level we are inadequate and that our failures render us unlovable and unacceptable.[2] When our failures are public, when we recognize our guilt and responsibility for them and when they have injured others we love, we find our failures touching us at the core of our being, forcing us to ask agonizing existential questions: "Who am I?" "What did I do wrong?" "What can I do now?" "What am I worth?"[3]

Failure on the Job

Often our failures and feelings of failure relate to our work. This is not surprising in American culture, where success is regularly tied to achievement, recognition, respect and wealth, and where a job is seen to be the primary source of these things. The words of pastor and author Robert Kemper reflect this reality: "To lose one's job is to be judged a failure. To lose one's work is to sense a loss of identity, status, and social relationships."[4]

We read in Genesis that when God created humanity, he gave us fruitful work to do. He entrusted our first parents—and through them the entire human race—with the responsibility of ruling the earth and filling it with his glory (Gen 1:28). Adam was commissioned to tend the Garden of Eden and to care for it (Gen 2:15). Before humanity fell into sin, God provided satisfying and fulfilling work for his image-bearers to do. Because the importance of work is God-ordained, it's not surprising that real and perceived failures in this area impact us deeply.

Such has been the case in our recent economic crisis. Some prominent corporations have failed—that is, gone into bankruptcy. Others have been weakened to the point where they had to be purchased by other institutions. And some others are still in business only because of massive government bailouts. In the minds of many, these failures are the fault of CEOs and other key executives. Whether this is actually the case can be answered only through extensive business analysis, coupled with significant soul searching by the key players involved.

At the very least, however, executives in these companies failed to meet the goals anticipated and expected by their boards and shareholders. And the effects of these failures are felt by huge numbers of people—the thousands of workers who lost their jobs, the stockholders whose investments lost their value and, in the cases of government bailouts, the American taxpayers who were required to foot the bill.

While these business failures are complex and open to multiple interpretations regarding responsibility and blame, the case of Bernard L. Madoff is a very clear-cut case of failure—in business, legal and ultimately moral senses. On December 11, 2008, Madoff was arrested by FBI agents and charged with turning his wealth-management business into a massive Ponzi scheme that defrauded thousands of investors of billions of dollars.[5] Three months later he pled guilty to eleven federal offenses, including securities fraud, wire fraud, mail fraud, money laundering and theft from an employee benefit fund. In his guilty plea, he admitted that the Ponzi scheme began in 1991 (though prosecutors claimed it actually began in the 1980s). A court-appointed trustee determined that the amount missing from client accounts (including fabricated gains) was almost sixty-five billion dollars. The actual losses to investors were estimated at eighteen billion.

On June 29, 2009, U.S. District Judge Denny Chin sentenced Madoff to the maximum sentence of 150 years in prison. He called Madoff's crimes "extraordinarily evil," "unprecedented" and "staggering." Madoff acknowledged that his guilt was inexcusable, saying,

> I cannot offer you an excuse for my behavior. How do you excuse betraying thousands of investors who entrusted me with their life savings? How do you excuse deceiving 200 employees who spent most of their working life with me? How do you excuse lying to a brother and two sons who

spent their entire lives helping to build a successful business? How do you excuse lying to a wife who stood by you for fifty years?

He concluded, "I will live with this pain, with this torment for the rest of my life."[6]

Much of the torment Madoff has experienced comes at a family level. The estrangement from his wife, Ruth, was evident from the statement she released after his sentencing: "I am embarrassed and ashamed. Like everyone else, I feel betrayed and confused. The man who committed this horrible fraud is not the man whom I have known for all these years."[7]

But things got worse. On the morning of December 11, 2010—the second anniversary of Madoff's arrest—his elder son, Mark Madoff, was found dead in his New York City apartment. The city medical examiner ruled the cause of his death as suicide by hanging. One can only begin to imagine the depth and intensity of guilt and remorse that Bernie Madoff must be experiencing.

On a much smaller and less public scale, Jim experienced a failure in business that impacted others. He was fired from two jobs prior to enrolling full time in graduate school. The first dismissal he attributed to the company being "screwed up." But even though the next company was dysfunctional as well, a second firing was harder to ignore. It made Jim look at himself more deeply.

Reflecting back, he could see how, in both job situations, his attitudes were directly involved. His pride led to fear, which in turn led him to function in self-protective ways characterized by lashing out at coworkers and even at his superiors. Believing these attitudes to be sinful and the cause, in part at least, for his dismissals has intensified Jim's sense of failure. But even harder for him has been the impact of the resulting financial insecurity on his wife. He says, "Thinking of this effect on her makes me feel more like a failure than any effect the losses had on me."

Samuel was an associate pastor of a local church. He was happily engaged in ministry there when a previously misdiagnosed bipolar disorder led to a series of actions that were at times odd and erratic and at other times immoral. These activities led the church's executive board to ask him to resign. As a result, Samuel lost his job, his home and then his marriage. Though he is now on medication that is proving effective in controlling his illness, he is painfully aware of where he has been, what he has done and what he has lost. While the issue of fault in Samuel's case is complex, owing to the interplay between mental illness and personal responsibility, in many other cases, there is very little doubt.

All too often people lose their jobs through no fault of their own. In December 2010, the unemployment rate in the United States stood at 9.4 percent. This number represents 14.5 million Americans who are out of work.[8] Clearly, the vast majority of these unemployed people were not responsible for losing their jobs. They bore the brunt of corporate layoffs or other economic factors. Yet many of them, no doubt, wonder if there was something they could have done to change the situation. All these people have experienced a kind of failure—a failure to meet their employment goals and to continue earning their wages. They are left not only with economic anxiety for themselves and their families, but also with the void of not having meaningful work to do.

The sense of failure for many continues long after the layoff. In December 2010, the number of long-term unemployed individuals (out of work for twenty-seven weeks or more) was 6.4 million (44.3 percent of the unemployed).[9] It is taking longer and longer for unemployed persons to find new positions. The competition for vacant positions is increasing with larger numbers of applicants.

For every person who gets a job, many others experience the disappointment of yet another rejection. Whether justified or not, feelings of failure abound.

Still others who are employed find themselves underemployed. Their jobs are not challenging, and their gifts are not being utilized to the fullest. Often they feel that their work is unrelated to any passion within their soul, and they view their work as not having any meaningful impact in the world. As a result, their work is unsatisfying.

Barb graduated from college with honors. She also graduated without a clear sense of what to do with her life. Those she sought counsel from encouraged her to look at what she was passionate about and to seek a way to pursue it. Good advice—except that being passionate about something was not even on Barb's radar. All the things she had been encouraged to do as she was growing up—get good grades, be involved in extracurricular activities, have friends, honor her parents, love God—didn't help her answer the fundamental question "What do you want to do? What are your passions?"

These doubts and insecurities were magnified intensely in Barb's mind and heart by a very difficult set of cards she was dealt in her family of origin. All of these things led her to believe she must protect herself. So, figuratively speaking, Barb wrapped herself in a cocoon. She took a variety of jobs to support herself, but often they were positions in which she was significantly underemployed.

She writes, "As a single woman, having a purposeful career is something I have longed for. I have wanted to be knowledgeable and respected in my field. I have wanted my work to be of value and to make a difference for good in the world." Yet this has not happened. Knowing that she has not lived the vocational life she longed for pains her deeply.

Failure at Home

Another significant area in which we experience failure and feelings of failure involves our family relationships.

Lori was engaged, four months away from her wedding, when she discovered that her fiancé had been cheating on her. There had been many warning signs that this wasn't a healthy relationship, but she had kept trying to make the relationship work, ignoring the counsel of others. The infidelity was the last straw, however, and Lori called off the engagement. Yet, even though this relationship ended due to the actions of her fiancé, Lori felt like a failure. She had tried to do everything "right" (go to couples counseling, ask others in the church to pray and so on), yet it still hadn't worked out.

Samantha has been married twice. Both of her husbands, in her words, proved "unable to be good partners or fathers." While she does not feel that the breakup of her marriages was sin on her part, she does grieve over the pain they have caused her and her daughters. At times she feels like she is experiencing symptoms of post-traumatic stress, and this definitely has impacted other relationships in her life.

Joy and her husband have been trying to conceive for almost five years. They have tried several medical treatments that have failed, and Joy has experienced a miscarriage and an ectopic pregnancy. She realizes that these matters are out of her control and that she's not responsible. Yet she reports that she still feels the failure very deeply and personally.

Martha is a middle-aged married woman who is haunted by an encounter she had with her father shortly before he died. It occurred in the spring of her senior year in high school as she was preparing for graduation. Her family was on the brink of a significant transition: her brother would be getting married in June of that year and she would soon leave for college.

Martha had a very active social life, and she and her friends were always out and about. One evening, as her dad was watching her get ready to go out for the evening, he begged her to stay home more. He looked very sad; in fact, he cried—something Martha had never seen him do. She was the apple of his eye, and though it pained her to see him so sad, she went out anyway—and she continued to do so all summer. In October of that year, Martha's dad died of a sudden, massive heart attack. Even though she looks back on her behavior more as immaturity and shortsightedness rather than as sin, she is haunted by the memory of that evening.

Sue has three children whom she and her husband diligently and prayerfully sought to raise to be followers of Christ. Two of her three children are, in her words, "on the path." But their eldest describes herself as a "non-practicing Christian." This is an ongoing source of pain and heartache for Sue and her husband. In retrospect, Sue recognizes that in their zeal to do everything "by the book," they tried to force their daughter into a box that didn't fit her. They failed to see her as an individual with her own needs and preferences. If they could do it over, she says, they would try to be more lenient in certain areas and celebrate her uniqueness, while at the same time seeking to inculcate their values into her life. While Sue certainly recognizes that their daughter is her own person and has made her own choices, Sue still feels the pain and wishes she and her husband could correct their mistakes.

Sometimes our failures impact us drastically. Such has been the case with several public figures whose failures have been widely reported. Consider the case of Tiger Woods. When he crashed his SUV outside his Isleworth, Florida, mansion at 2:25 a.m. on the morning of November 27, 2009, his carefully crafted image began to unravel with devastating speed. Within weeks, the number of women who had either come forward or been identified by others as Woods's mistresses reached double digits. A leave of absence from professional golf, inpatient treatment for sex addiction, and the loss of lucrative endorsement deals from Gatorade, Accenture and AT&T soon followed.[10] But the impact on Woods's wife, Elin, has been perhaps the most devastating of all. Their divorce was finalized on August 23, 2010.

Of course, Woods is not alone in experiencing the impact of a sex scandal. The affair of former Democratic presidential candidate John Edwards with former aide Rielle Hunter and his attempts to cover up both the relationship and the out-of-wedlock child he fathered not only cost him his political future, it also cost him his marriage. In January 2010, Elizabeth Edwards legally separated from her husband, and they remained separated until Elizabeth's death in December 2010. The depth of their estrangement was indicated by Elizabeth's will. She left everything to her children, and her estranged husband was not mentioned at all.

Governor Mark Sanford of South Carolina was not forced from office after his secret trip to Buenos Aires to be with his Argentine mistress became public, but his political future is in shambles. And his marriage to Jenny ended after she filed for divorce. Elliot Spitzer was forced to resign in disgrace as the governor of New York after his involvement in a prostitution service became public. At the time of this writing, he remains married to his wife, Silda, but her wounds and those of their children are undoubtedly deep.

In each of these cases (and the list, unfortunately, could go on and on), the men experiencing a very public moral failure suffered professional loss. But the pain experienced by their wives and families runs every bit as deep, if not deeper.

Failure in Relationship with God

As Christians, we also experience failure in our relationship with God. Some, though not all, of the failures cited above reflect a level of moral failure in work and family life that Scripture would call sin. But there can be disobedience and a lack of faithfulness to God in other areas of life as well. Significant and prominent leaders of the people of God are not exempt; there is nothing about a leadership position that inherently makes one faithful to God.

King David is a classic and tragic example of this. He was a towering figure in the Old Testament, referred to as a "man after [God's] own heart" (1 Sam 13:14; Acts 13:22). David's reign as king was the high point of the Israelite monarchy. He was the recipient of God's covenant promises (2 Sam 7:1-17) and became the one who foreshadowed the coming "Son of David," Jesus.

But Scripture is brutally honest in describing David's greatest failure. Second Samuel 11 describes a time one spring when David remained at home in Jerusalem after sending his armies off to battle under the leadership of Joab. From the roof of his palace, he saw Bathsheba, a very beautiful woman, bathing. Even after he found out that she was a married woman, he continued to lust after her. The pressures of his reign were great. Surely he was entitled to some pleasure. He was the king, after all. Accustomed to having his own way, David sent for her. She was brought to him, and he slept with her. After that, Bathsheba went home, and David thought his sexual indiscretion was over and no one would be the wiser.

However, Bathsheba became pregnant. And when she sent word of it to David, he was faced with a crisis. Because her husband, Uriah, was on the battlefront, it would soon be evident to all that Uriah was not the father. David feared that further investigation would ensue and would uncover his adultery. So he did what we all so often do when we have sinned: he initiated a cover-up. He sent for Uriah from the front and encouraged him to go home to his wife, Bathsheba, clearly hoping that he would sleep with her and thus the pregnancy would be traced to Uriah.

But Uriah didn't do what David expected of him. He refused to sleep with his wife while the other soldiers were sleeping in tents at the battlefront. He was unwilling to violate the customary abstinence required of soldiers on their mission (1 Sam 21:5). When additional attempts to have Uriah sleep with Bathsheba failed, David knew he needed to take stronger measures. He sent Uriah back to the front with instructions for Joab to put Uriah into such a dangerous position that it would ensure his death. Joab obeyed these instructions, and Uriah was killed in battle.

When Bathsheba received the news, she mourned for her husband. Then David took her into his home as his wife (one of several of his wives, it must be said). And she bore him a son.

David's sin occurred on many fronts: lust, coveting a woman who was already married, abuse of power to coerce Bathsheba into his bed, adultery, lying, murder, increased polygamy. Second Samuel ends with one of the greatest understatements in all of Scripture: "But the thing David had done displeased the LORD" (2 Sam 11:27).

In the New Testament, Peter is another example of a leader of God's people who fell into sin and failure. He was a central figure—the leader of the twelve apostles, their spokesman on the day of Pentecost and the dominant figure in the early church in Jerusalem. But he was also a deeply flawed follower of Christ who had failed on numerous occasions.

Immediately after his monumental confession of faith in Christ as God's Messiah, Peter was aghast when Jesus began to predict his future sufferings. Peter tried to dissuade him from this course, only to have Jesus rebuke him, calling him a mouthpiece of Satan and a stumbling block to him (Mt 16:16, 23).[11]

After Jesus' death, resurrection and ascension, Peter was used mightily by God to lead the church in Jerusalem and to pioneer the spread of the gospel to Gentiles (Cornelius and his household, Acts 10:1-48). But even after such ministry "successes," he did not al-

ways live up to the truth he knew. On one such occasion, he with-
drew from eating with Gentile believers in Antioch. Sensing that
the heart of the gospel was being jeopardized, Paul "opposed him
to his face" and issued a stinging rebuke to Peter (Gal 2:11-14).
But neither of these incidents compared with what was unques-
tionably Peter's bitterest failure. It occurred on the night before
Jesus died. The Master himself had predicted that all his disciples
would fall away. With characteristic bravado, Peter told the Lord,
"Even if all fall away on account of you, I never will." Jesus knew
what would happen later that very day. "Truly I tell you, this very
night, before the rooster crows, you will disown me three times"
(Mt 26:33-34). Peter continued to protest, but subsequent events
would prove that his confidence in his own persevering faithfulness to Jesus was misplaced.[12]

While Jesus was before the Sanhedrin, Peter was sitting in the
courtyard of the high priest. The night was cold, and he was warm-
ing himself beside a fire. Three different times he was approached
by servants of the high priest, asking if he was a follower of Jesus.
Three different times, Peter denied it, ultimately even calling
down curses on himself in an attempt to make the servant believe
him (Mt 26:74).

No doubt, Peter was afraid that what was happening to Jesus
could also happen to him if his allegiance to Jesus was known.
But the threat against Peter at that moment was quite small. He
had boastfully declared to Jesus earlier that day that even if he
had to die with Christ, he would never disown him. And yet,
when faced with the questions of a servant girl, he willingly dis-
owned his master.

Then the rooster crowed. Luke records that, at that moment,
the Lord turned and "looked straight at Peter" (Lk 22:61). Scripture records that Peter went outside and wept bitterly. Such was
the sting of this most grievous failure.

Peter is not the only Christian leader to experience failure in a relationship with Jesus. Present-day leaders of the Christian church are no strangers to failure. Sometimes their sins are sexual—as with the recent sexual abuse scandals of Roman Catholic priests or the double life of Reverend Ted Haggard or the abundant abuse of Internet pornography by evangelical pastors.[13] Other sins involve money—either greed and materialism at the personal or family level, or financial mismanagement in official capacities. Or they may involve the abuse of power.[14]

But other sins infect the church as well. Consider the sin of racism. The well-known truism that the most segregated hour in the United States is 11:00 on Sunday morning has been well documented by Michael Emerson and Christian Smith in their groundbreaking book *Divided by Faith*.[15] Philip Yancey puts a human face on this devastating moral failure among Christians in his book *What's So Amazing About Grace?* Breaking the all-too-common taboo against disclosing our failures and sins, Yancey wrote very honestly, "I grew up a racist." He described the "perfectly legal form of apartheid" he experienced growing up.

> Stores in downtown Atlanta had three rest rooms: "White Men," "White Women," and "Colored." Gas stations had two drinking fountains, one for "whites" and one for "colored." Motels and restaurants served white patrons only, and when the Civil Rights Act made such discrimination illegal, many owners shuttered their establishments.[16]

This was the cultural air Yancey breathed, so that it was not unusual for him to buy, with money earned from his paper route, an ax handle that was a replica of those used to beat back civil rights demonstrators. His cultural racism took on a theological foundation through the teachings and the actions of his church. It not only taught a twisted justification for racism, it also actively rejected the requests for membership of the very few African Americans who sought to join its number. (One was a student at Carver Bible Institute, Tony Evans, currently a prominent African American pastor and speaker.) Yancey concluded,

> Today as I look back on my childhood I feel shame, remorse, and also repentance. It took years for God to break through my armor of blatant racism—I wonder if any of us sheds its more subtle forms—and I now see that sin as one of the most malevolent, with the greatest societal impact. I hear much talk these days about the underclass and the crisis in urban America. Experts blame in turn drugs, a decline in values, poverty, and the breakdown in the nuclear family. I wonder if all those problems are consequences of a deeper, under-lying cause: our centuries-old sin of racism.[17]

In these and so many other ways, the failures of Christians to live as God would have them—individually and collectively—abound.

The Inevitability of Failure

I hope that the preceding discussion has illustrated the fact that our failures are many and varied. They can be big or small. They can be private and personal, or they can become headlines on the national news. Failures come with varying levels of moral respon-sibility, including failures that are clearly our fault, failures that are clearly the fault of someone else, and much more complex ex-periences in which responsibility is borne by multiple parties.

But failure is inevitable. Whereas many of our failures can and must be avoided, to one extent or another, we all fail. In her com-mencement address at Harvard University in 2008, J. K. Rowl-ing, celebrated author of the Harry Potter series, told the gradu-ating students, "Some failure in life is inevitable. It is impossible to live without failing at something, unless you live so cautiously that you might as well not have lived at all—in which case, you fail by default."[18]

Some of this inevitability of failure comes from our cultural expectations of success. Our cultural milieu is shaped in many ways by the advertising industry. Again and again we are told in a whole host of ways that the "good life" is achieved by the acquisition and consumption of certain products. Daily we are bombarded with massive amounts of alluring images that promise us everything from popularity to serenity, power to prestige, sexual fulfillment to the perfect family. We are told, sometimes subtly and often blatantly, that we can be "better"—more beautiful, more powerful, more envied, more successful—if only we buy these things. This all-pervasive advertising is designed to make us feel dissatisfied and unfulfilled with our current state of consumption.

But the promises of a better life and a better self are ones that no consumer product can fulfill. American consumer culture and the advertising industry that drives it are purveyors of what Jesus referred to as "the deceitfulness of wealth" (Mk 4:19). Wealth is deceitful when it promises what it cannot deliver. And Jesus teaches that this deceitfulness of wealth is one of the thorns that can choke out the good seed of the Word of God in our lives.

Equally deceitful are the alluring promises made by popularity, prestige and power. None of them can satisfy the deepest desires of our hearts. God has created us for so much more. He has set eternity in our hearts (Eccles 3:11), such that we will be satisfied only by God himself. In our eager willingness to look to wealth, power and prestige as the pathway to success and satisfaction, we are merely repeating the idolatry of ancient Israel. In the powerful words of Jeremiah, we have forsaken our God, the only spring of living water that will truly satisfy us, and have instead dug our own cisterns— "broken cisterns that cannot hold water" (Jer 2:11-13).

Is it any wonder that we feel a sense of failure when the things we so eagerly strive for in the pursuit of success fail us? The deceitfulness of wealth, prestige and power contribute to the virtual inevitability of feelings of failure.

Competitiveness also makes a sense of failure inevitable. If only those who rise to the top are considered successes, if Vince Lombardi is right and winning is the only thing, then by definition there can be very few successes. That is certainly true in sports. Professional and college sports teams rarely repeat as champions. Last year's success is no guarantee of this year's. Does a failure to win this year really mean a team and its players and coaches are failures?

Competition flourishes in other areas as well. In 2008, *People* magazine voted Hugh Jackman as its "sexiest man alive." What does that mean for every other man? The *Chicago Tribune* reported that 2007's winner, George Clooney, called Jackman to "complain" that he "started this big campaign . . . and took the title away from me."[19] Clooney's comments were no doubt made in jest, but they do reflect the reality that only one person can win the title in any given year.

Failure—real and perceived—is not just a twenty-first-century American phenomenon. The Gospels are very honest about the failures of the first followers of Jesus. New Testament theologian Scot McKnight notes that they record a consistent pattern of failure on the part of the disciples: they failed to understand Jesus' teachings; they became filled with fear rather than faith in a boat with Jesus during a storm; they didn't understand how Jesus could provide for others; they struggled to follow their Master in his acceptance of Gentiles and of children; and they fell asleep at the point of Jesus' greatest need, when he had specifically asked them to stay awake so they could pray.[20] McKnight argues that this pattern of imperfection indicates that disciples of Jesus are not sinless. Failure is a part of what it means for human beings to follow

Jesus. Even when we make progress in becoming more and more like Christ, we never outgrow failure altogether.[21]

Success in God's eyes is not the absence of failure. Rather, it involves applying the grace of God to our failures, so that we can continue to grow in faithfulness to him.[22]

Unhealthy Responses to Failure

Unfortunately, not all of us respond well to the failures in our lives. The following is a representative, but surely not exhaustive, list of some unhealthy responses to failure.

Denial. Failure can be so threatening to our sense of self, to our vision of ourselves as competent and worthwhile, that it often seems easier to deny that it has happened. We rationalize it away, failing to take responsibility where it exists. We compare ourselves to others, and if we can find someone else who is less successful than we are, we deem ourselves to be better in comparison. Often we try to escape from our failures by immersing ourselves in alcohol, various drugs, work or hobbies.

But all these attempts to deny the failures we have experienced are never totally successful. Even our best efforts to run away from them are futile in the end. Sooner or later, we have to deal with failure. In the final analysis, denial is a retreat from reality that proves to be a dead end.

Silence. When we find our failures staring us in the face so relentlessly that we cannot deny them, we may try to hide them from others. We feel that if no one else knows, we will not be a failure in others' eyes. So we clam up. We get quiet. We don't talk about our failures with anyone else. Sometimes we are not even honest about them with God.

Yet the very silence that we feel will protect us ends up being counterproductive. Scripture calls us to confess our sins—to God and to one another. Again, not all failures are sinful, but those that are need to be confessed. Confessing our sins to God leads to his forgiveness and to the purifying work of his Spirit (1 Jn 1:9). Confession to trusted brothers and sisters (Jas 5:16) can be a powerful means of grace; God is pleased to communicate his mercy through his people. Such honesty is crucial for us to be able to forgive ourselves. As Lewis Smedes perceptively wrote, "Without honesty, self-forgiveness is psychological hocus-pocus. The rule is: we cannot really forgive ourselves unless we look at the failure in our past and call it by its right name."[23]

Honesty and openness have value even for failures that aren't the result of sin. They enable us to continue walking in the light, even as our God is in the light (1 Jn 1:7). Refusing to keep silent robs our failures of their power to dominate us at subjective and emotional levels. Failures that we refuse to acknowledge are failures that will continue to haunt us.

Paralyzing fear. Some people respond to the pain of failure with fear of failing again. This paralyzes them and makes them unwilling to take risks. They become like the servant in Jesus' parable of the talents, who buried the money entrusted to him by his master in the ground, lest he lose any of it and then have to face his master (Mt 25:18, 24-30).

People paralyzed by the fear of failure withdraw from relationships to guard their hearts against rejection. They refuse to take risks in their work lives. "What if it doesn't turn out and I experience failure rather than success?" Rather than being liberated by the love and acceptance of God our Father, they cocoon themselves away from all risk.

But such self-protectiveness, while guarding us against the possibility of certain kinds of failures, guarantees other kinds. Cocooning ourselves does not lead to faithfulness to the Lord. We cannot truly love God and our neighbors if we are always guarding our hearts and refusing to take risks. We may well avoid some failures, but a life characterized by fear of failure will never be filled with success.

Continuing to do the same things. Albert Einstein famously defined insanity as "doing the same thing over and over again and expecting different results."[24] This is how some respond to failure. While many of our failures are exceedingly complex and involve issues that will take a long time to understand and correct, some of them are the result of doing unwise, unhealthy and very preventable things over and over again. No doubt some of the ignorance involved is owed to our finite nature. But surely some ignorance is correctable, and God would have us learn and take the hard road of change.

When this change involves turning from sinful choices and behaviors and turning instead to the path of righteousness, Scripture calls it repentance. This repentance is the gift of God and the pathway to life.[25] But even if there is no sin involved in our failures, an unwillingness to learn from them and change our behavior is an unhealthy way to cope with failure.

Identifying ourselves as failures. Consciously or subconsciously we sometimes allow our failures to form our identity. We move from admitting that we have failed to believing ourselves to *be* failures. We define ourselves and our lives in terms of the bankruptcy, the divorce, the unemployment or our parenting weaknesses.

What a far cry from the identity our heavenly Father wants us to have, experience and live out—that of being a beloved child of his forever! What a tragedy it is when, rather than experiencing God's forgiveness and redemption of our failures, we take our identity from them.

Denial, silence, paralyzing fear, unwillingness to change, identity formation—these are all unhealthy responses to failure.[26] But what should we do instead? How should we respond to the inevitable failures in our lives? We'll turn our attention to this question in the next chapter.

5

Grappling with Failure Theologically

ॐ

According to Scripture, a crucial component of God-honoring living is clear and accurate thinking. How we think matters.

This truth was affirmed by the apostle Paul in his letter to the Romans. He urged his brothers and sisters to respond to God's mercy by continually offering their bodies to God as living sacrifices. He assured them that this lifestyle of faithful dedication constitutes spiritual worship that is pleasing to the Lord (Rom 12:1). But such a wholehearted offering of our whole lives to God requires an inner transformation. Paul wrote, "Do not conform to the pattern of this world, but be transformed by the renewing of your mind. Then you will be able to test and approve what God's will is—his good, pleasing and perfect will" (Rom 12:2).

What will transform our lives out of a downward spiral of conformity to a world system that stands in opposition to God and his values? What will bring us into greater conformity to the image and likeness of Christ? The renewing of our minds. This involves learning and internalizing in ever-greater measure the truths of Scripture. It comes from meditating on God's Word, reflecting on it again and again, until our whole way of thinking becomes more and more in line with the thoughts and values God has revealed. To be sure, the truth we learn from Scripture must be lived out. Knowledge gained for its own sake merely "puffs up" (1 Cor 8:1). God is not at all interested in us acquiring an ever-expanding cognitive reservoir of theological truths that we have absolutely no intention of putting into practice. But we can never live out truths that we don't know. While we are never finished until we apply the truths of Scripture to our lives and our relationships, step one must always involve learning them clearly and accurately. Such knowing is supremely practical and relevant.[1]

This chapter and the next will provide us with much opportunity to have our minds renewed by the truth of God in Scripture. As we meditate on God's truth about our failures, we will find that it is filled with grace. Even as John described Jesus coming into the world "full of grace and truth" (Jn 1:14), so we find that the Scriptures speak to the failure in our lives with "grace and truth." The five truths we'll explore are truths of grace.

Truth of Grace 1: Not All Failures Are Sinful

As we grapple with our experience of failure, we must begin where the Bible begins—with creation. The first thing God wants to tell us about himself is that he is the Creator of everything that exists (Gen 1:1). Equally so, the very first thing Scripture tells us about ourselves as human beings is that we are creatures created by our almighty and loving Creator in his own image (Gen 1:26-27).

Being created in the image of God is a wonderful gift of his grace. The image is both a status of dignity and value bestowed on every human being and a standard to which God calls all humans in their lives and relationships.[2] It forms the theological basis for universal human rights and for our ethical responsibilities to one another. It sets a trajectory of life and community for all of us to pursue as humans, both individually and collectively. But for our purposes, what is most important is that "God *created* human beings in his own image" (Gen 1:27, emphasis added). The truth is that we humans are creatures—finite creatures. As such, we are profoundly different from our infinite Creator. I remember a poster of a beautiful sunset that had the following caption: "Two Foundational Facts of Human Enlightenment: (1) There is a God. (2) You are not him!"

It's good to be finite. God the Creator is infinite. We humans, on the other hand, are not. God is infinite in power, and we humans are weak and impotent in comparison. Even the most powerful human leader pales in comparison with the omnipotent God. Our Creator is infinite in knowledge and wisdom; we are very limited in knowledge[3] and our best efforts at "wisdom" are so often filled with folly. While God is infinitely self-sufficient, we humans are utterly dependent on God to give to us "life and breath and everything else" (Acts 17:25). Our God is sovereign and reigns supreme over all his creation. We humans, on the other hand, are clay in the hands of the divine Potter.

Many of us react negatively to the reality of such limitations. We want to be in control of our lives and our destinies. We don't want to be dependent on anyone else. We long to have power and knowledge in abundant measure. But God's perspective on human finiteness is very different from our own. Prior to the creation of human beings, God considered his creation to be "good" (Gen 1:10, 12, 18, 21, 25). But after his creation of human beings in his own image, God pronounced his creation to be "very good" (Gen 1:31). God takes delight in his image bearers, in all their created humanness—including their finiteness.

Human finiteness is not a problem for God. It is a central part of his "very good" creation.[4] Yet it is this finiteness that accounts for many of the failures we experience.

Every one of our decisions is made with very limited knowledge of the future. As a result, many of them don't turn out the way we had hoped. This does not necessarily mean that any one of these decisions was the wrong one. Our decision may very well have been the wisest possible one based on what we knew or could predict at the time. But many of our decisions can have negative consequences.

Several years ago, Bill and Sue bought a condominium. It was a spacious and attractive unit in a good neighborhood, close to their jobs. When they bought it, the real estate market was strong and the resale value was high. It seemed a wise decision for them to make such an investment. When Bill took a new job in a different city and they moved, he and Sue put their condo on the market. While they knew that it was a difficult time to sell, they felt that the new job was the right one for them. They priced their unit accordingly, and their realtor took aggressive measures to market it. However, no one foresaw the collapse of the housing market in the months to come. Even though Bill and Sue kept reducing their asking price, they had few showings and no offers. Throughout this process, they were living with other family members, while continuing to pay the mortgage on a home they were not living in.

Meanwhile, Bill's new job turned out to be exceedingly difficult. After several months, it became apparent that it was not a good fit. The need to find a new job, coupled with the failure of their condo to sell, prompted Bill and Sue to move back into their original condo.

The year was very difficult for them in many ways. But were their decisions about the job and their condo "failures"? Certainly not in any blameworthy way! In one sense they "failed" to accomplish their original vocational and lifestyle goals, and they might second-guess some of the specifics of their decision-making. And throughout the process, they no doubt felt frustration, uncertainty, discouragement and perhaps some shame.[5] But Bill and Sue were not at all at fault for the repercussions of their decisions. Whatever emotions they might have felt, guilt should not have been one of them.

Just as we humans have limited knowledge, we also have limited power. We just can't do everything. We cannot keep every ball in the air. If we try, some will inevitably come crashing down. But this is not a bad thing. If human finiteness is a God-designed element of a created universe that he declared to be "very good," we too should accept our finiteness and its inherent limitations. This is part of responding gratefully to our Creator.

Author Jean Blomquist declares that one of the most significant discoveries she has made is that incompleteness is not the same thing as failure.[6] Or more precisely, it is not a morally blameworthy failure. Even if we experience a "failure" as a result of decisions made with incomplete knowledge or because we did not have enough power to handle every possible contingency, such incompleteness is not sinful.

The inevitability of risk. Virtually every decision of any substance has implications for our future. Decisions involve risk precisely because our human knowledge is finite and limited. There is always the possibility that our decisions and actions will end up involving injury or loss—to ourselves or to others. And this is by God's design. In the vast majority of cases, he has not decided to reveal to us what will happen in the future.[7] So we need to make the best and wisest decisions we can and to trust God with the risks involved.

Many of us are very risk averse. We want life to be safe and secure, familiar and comfortable. When the reality of risk presents itself, we instinctively shrink back, seeking to protect ourselves and our loved ones from any possible adverse consequences. Sometimes this is wise. Not every risk is worth taking. But it is impossible to avoid risk completely. And many times it is right to take risks when following God's direction.

One of the greatest heroines in all of Scripture is Esther, a Jewish exile who rose to the position of queen in the Persian Empire. She was faced with a crisis due to the actions of Haman, one of the chief advisers to the Persian King Xerxes. Haman hated Esther's uncle, Mordecai, and indeed all the Jewish refugees. He persuaded King Xerxes to issue a decree that they all be exterminated. The king agreed to this decree, not realizing that his queen, Esther, was Jewish.

What was Queen Esther to do? She knew the Persian law that said she could not approach the king without being summoned by him. If she did, she would be put to death, unless the king specifically pardoned her by lifting his golden scepter. But she also knew that the lives of her people were at stake. Mordecai asked her to take the risk of approaching the king on behalf of her people and the cause of her God. Esther's reply to Mordecai was, "Go, gather together all the Jews who are in Susa, and fast for me. Do not eat or drink for three days, night or day. I and my attendants will fast as you do. When this is done, I will go to the king, even though it is against the law. And if I perish, I perish" (Esther 4:16).

Esther did not know what the ultimate outcome of her action would be. She had no special revelation from God as to what would happen. She had to make a decision on the basis of wisdom and love for her people, even though her knowledge of the future was limited. She made her decision and handed the results over to God, saying, "If I perish, I perish." Often, it is right to risk for the cause of God.

In the end, King Xerxes did respond to Esther's request. He changed his mind and saved the Jews. But the "rightness" of a risk is not determined by a happy ending. In the New Testament, Stephen took a risk by publicly indicting Israel for its long history of resisting the work of God (Acts 7:2-53). His preaching so infuriated the Jewish authorities that he was stoned and became the first Christian martyr (Acts 7:54-60). He, too, was right to risk for the cause of God, even though his vindication would come only in eternity.[8]

Risks are inevitable for us due to our creation as finite beings. We can never eliminate risk altogether.[9] Attempting to do so is a very real denial of our humanity[10] as well as a lack of trust in God's ordering of our lives. But the inevitability of risk does mean that we will often experience failure due to unintended consequences of our decisions—even the wisest of them.

Created to be unique. Many of our feelings of failure come from comparisons we make with other people. If we believe ourselves to be less wealthy or popular, or to possess less prestige or power, we may think of ourselves as failures. Sometimes our comparisons are based on decisions made or work done. But often we compare ourselves to others based on gifts given by God in creation. We focus on physical attractiveness, intelligence, personality type or athletic ability. And if we feel that we do not measure up to others around us, we consider ourselves to be failures.

Sometimes these feelings of failure are compounded by the green-eyed monster, envy. Susan and I have experienced this in our relationship. We are very different people in terms of basic personality types. I am an analytical thinker; Susan leads from her gut. She is quick to speak and to decide; I move at a much slower (glacial?) pace. She is relationally intuitive and sensitive, and I am working on those skills.

For the most part, we appreciate our differences and the ways they enable us to complement each other. At our best, we are content with the way God has made each of us, and we appreciate the very real strengths of our spouse. But at our worst, we can each get down on ourselves because we are not like the other. We can be unsatisfied with the way God made us. We compare, and we covet what God has been pleased to give to the other. I can regularly beat myself up for relational faux pas or for not speaking up on an issue when it is called for (in other words, for not being like Susan). Susan can get down on herself for leading with her gut and for not being the kind of think-before-you-speak person she wants to be (in other words, for not being like me). These comparisons can come out sideways in the form of angry words or moody silences that damage our relationship.

Instead of comparing and envying, we should rejoice in our differences. The God of creation does not want his human image bearers to be identical. His desire is that each and every human be unique. God makes humans to be both male and female (Gen 1:27).[11] He makes us different and unique in height and weight, in hair color and skin color. God gives to us different personalities and temperaments. He creates us with varying levels of athletic and intellectual ability. While many of these attributes can be developed and enhanced through our own efforts, it is also true that, because of God's work in creation, there is a very real "givenness" to who we are. Scripture assures us that, with the deepest possible wisdom and love, God created each of us the way we are. Our response should be that of David, who marveled at the way God had fashioned him in his mother's womb and then burst out in praise to his Creator: "I praise you because I am fearfully and wonderfully made" (Ps 139:14). These are words that every human being can rightly say.

When we are tempted to think that God made a mistake or two when he created us the way he did, the testimony of Scripture can renew our minds. God is our Creator. He has made us according to his wisdom and love. As a result, we can accept ourselves and thank him for making us the way he did.[12]

To be sure, some of our "givens" from creation may put us at a disadvantage in certain areas compared to others around us. A person who, because of his or her God-given biological makeup, needs relatively little sleep to function well will no doubt be able to produce more in those extra hours of wakefulness than others like me who need six to eight hours of sleep per night. To the extent that our understanding of success and failure is competitive and to the extent that our significant others evaluate us on the basis of these "givens" of creation, we might think of ourselves as failures. But if God is our ultimate significant other, if his work and his perspective are indeed the most important in our lives, we can accept ourselves for who he has made us to be.[13] Because we trust in the wisdom and love of God, we can celebrate both our uniqueness and that of others, even when they "surpass" us in some ways. Success in the eyes of God is not a win-lose proposition; all of God's children can be successful in his eyes through their faithfulness. None of us should experience a sense of failure because of how we were made.

Living in a fallen world. There is one additional truth we must consider as we come to grips with the fact that not all failures are sinful: the world we live in is fallen. Scripture tells us that after our first parents fell into rebellion and sin, the entire created universe was cursed by God (Gen 3:17-19; Rom 8:19-21). As a result, the world in which we live impacts us in various dysfunctional and detrimental ways. We can experience many of these effects as "failures" of sorts. But they have nothing to do with specific sin in our lives.

In chapter four, we considered the experience of Joy. She and her husband had been trying to conceive for almost five years—without success. While admitting that her inability to get pregnant made her at times feel as if she had failed, she nevertheless realized that she was not responsible. Her "felt" failure was not the result of sin. It was the result of living in a fallen world.

Living in a fallen world means living in relationship with other human beings who are also fallen. Life after the Fall means not only that we all sin but also that we are all sinned against by others. At times we can subjectively experience the impact of the sins of others against us as failures. Lori, you may remember, ended her engagement when she discovered that her fiancé had been unfaithful to her. Samantha went through two divorces. In each case, it was the man's inability to be a good partner or father that brought about the breakup. For Barb, a very dysfunctional family of origin and being deeply sinned against by members of that family contributed significantly to an inability to know what she was passionate about when she entered the job market after college. This contributed greatly to her ongoing vocational dissatisfaction and feelings of failure.

In each of these cases, it was the sinful actions of others that significantly impacted the person who felt the "failure" so deeply. The emotional trauma is real and the need to cope is great for these individuals. But a crucial step in the process is to realize that being sinned against is not sinful. Anger, sadness, frustration and many other emotions may be felt, but guilt need not be one of them. As we continue to be renewed in our minds by the truth that not all our failures are sinful, we can move beyond false guilt and deal more constructively with other emotions and other dimensions of our experience.

Giving grace to ourselves. If all of this is true, how should we respond? We can prayerfully seek to internalize the truth that not all failures are sinful. We can seek to increase our capacity to discern the difference between regret and guilt and to distinguish between real and perceived failures.[14] We can seek more and more to accept ourselves as the unique beings God has created us to be. In addition, we can grow in one other crucial response: we can learn to give grace to ourselves—or perhaps more accurately, to allow ourselves to receive and experience God's grace.

As our Creator, God rejoices in and celebrates the finite and unique creatures he has made us to be, far more than we do. The psalmist who wrote Psalm 103 says, "As a father has compassion on his children, so the LORD has compassion on those who fear him; for he knows how we are formed, he remembers that we are dust" (Ps 103:13-14). God is fully aware of how he has made us. He knows how we are formed—as finite and dependent creatures. He knows we have limited knowledge and power. He knows that our lifespan is so small compared to eternity. He knows how we measure up with others. And precisely because God knows us completely, he has compassion on us.

We all need to be like our heavenly Father and have compassion on ourselves. How different our experience in life would be if we could learn to accept ourselves and live with humility and patience in our finiteness.[15] While we will, no doubt, regret those decisions that didn't turn out as we had hoped and while we still may experience feelings of disappointment and frustration, giving grace to ourselves will transform that experience. No longer will the struggle against guilt be dominant. Rather, the grace of God will be paramount. As we accept ourselves for the finite and unique persons God has made us to be, we are able to reach out to others in all their uniqueness as well.

This is the way of faithfulness to God our Creator. This is the way of success in his eyes.

Truth of Grace 2: All Sinful Failures Are Forgiven by God

While we can and must affirm that not every failure is sinful, we must also be honest enough to say that some are. Both Scripture and experience confirm that all of us are sinners. Paul's testimony that "all have sinned and fall short of the glory of God" rings true in our consciences (Rom 3:23).[16] In this sense, we must say that all of us have failed again and again. We have failed to love God and love our neighbors. We have failed to live like Christ in the world. And often the guilt and shame we feel over these sinful failures makes them especially difficult to cope with.[17] But the Bible is filled with good news for sinful people like us. Throughout the Scriptures, we find an insistent and persistent proclamation: Our God forgives the sins of his people!

A God who forgives. This reality is at the heart of a recurring Old Testament description of God that formed the centerpiece of the faith of the people of Israel. After God's deliverance of the Israelites from slavery in Egypt, he gave them his law on Mount Sinai. But not long after receiving this law, Israel broke the first two of the Ten Commandments by making and worshiping a golden calf. Yet God forgave their sin, and he proclaimed that such compassionate and gracious forgiveness is at the heart of his very nature. God described himself as "the LORD, the LORD, the compassionate and gracious God, slow to anger, abounding in love and faithfulness, maintaining love to thousands, and forgiving wickedness, rebellion and sin" (Ex 34:6-7).[18] So important is this description that it is repeatedly used, in whole or in part, throughout the Old Testament to describe the God of Israel (Neh 9:17; Ps 103:8-10; Joel 2:13; Jon 4:2).

In Old Testament times, forgiveness was achieved through a series of sacrifices. Gracious gifts of God though they were, these animal sacrifices were never enough to deal with sin fully and finally (as argued in Heb 9–10). So God declared that he would establish a new covenant in which he would permanently deal with the sin of his people. As a result, God promised, "I will forgive their wickedness and will remember their sins no more" (Jer 31:34).

According to the New Testament, this new covenant was inaugurated through Jesus' death on the cross. On the night before he died, Jesus looked ahead to what would happen the next day as he instituted the Lord's Supper. Over the cup, he said, "This is my blood of the covenant, which is poured out for many for the forgiveness of sins" (Mt 26:28). The fullness of God's forgiveness of his people has been given to us in and through Christ (Eph 4:32). This is the heart of the gospel. God has acted decisively in Christ to deal with the issue of sin and to reconcile estranged human beings to himself. And he takes great joy in the intimacy that comes from this reconciliation.[19]

Justified by his grace. The apostle Paul spoke of this full and free forgiveness by using the language of justification. In his letter to the Romans, he followed his description of our universal experience of falling short of what God wants with the good news of his justifying grace in Christ.

> For all have sinned and fall short of the glory of God, and all are justified freely by his grace through the redemption that came by Christ Jesus. God presented Christ as a sacrifice of atonement, through the shedding of his blood—to be received by faith . . . so as to be just and the one who justifies those who have faith in Jesus. (Rom 3:23-26)

The language of justification is related to that of righteousness. In biblical usage, it is a legal term, speaking of the action of a judge to declare a person to be righteous.[20] When God justifies sinful men and women who have faith in Jesus, he is declaring them to be not guilty of their sin, but rather to be righteous because of Christ.[21] This is a free gift of God's love and grace, received by faith alone and not earned by us in any way.

God forgives our sin because of the death of Christ.[22] Christ paid the penalty for sin, so that God can rightly declare all those who trust him to be righteous in him. There is a great exchange. Our sin is transferred to Christ so that he might pay the penalty for it, and his righteousness is transferred to us that we might enjoy its benefits.[23] "God made [Christ] who had no sin to be sin for us, so that in him we might become the righteousness of God" (2 Cor 5:21).

The benefits of justification. God's justifying grace brings amazing benefits to the children of God. Central to these benefits is the gift of peace with God. Romans 5:1 says, "Therefore, since we have been justified through faith, we have peace with God through our Lord Jesus Christ." Rather than our sin being a source of estrangement and alienation between ourselves and God, now because of Christ there is peace. The war is over!

My father was among those U.S. Marines who were training in the Pacific for a possible invasion of the Japanese mainland during the latter days of World War II. Imagine his emotions on August 15, 1945, when he and the other soldiers heard the news that the emperor of Japan had accepted the Allied terms of surrender, bringing World War II to an end. What joy and relief he must have felt, knowing that he would no longer have to face Japanese soldiers as his enemies. His life and his health would no longer be threatened by hostility. There was peace.

So it is with us and God. His righteous and holy wrath against our sin has been fully satisfied because of Christ. And we are at peace—not the fragile kind of peace that is too often the norm in wartorn areas of the world. The peace that God proclaims between himself and his children is permanent and unshakable. No sin on our part can ever undo it.[24]

Never again should any child of God fear his condemnation. "Therefore, there is now no condemnation for those who are in Christ Jesus" (Rom 8:1). The ultimate verdict is already in. The judge has declared the final outcome. Even though we are sinners, God has declared us to be forgiven and righteous because of Christ. And nothing can ever change that fact. "Who will bring any charge against those whom God has chosen? It is God who justifies. Who then can condemn? No one. Christ Jesus, who died—more than that, who was raised to life—is at the right hand of God and is also interceding for us" (Rom 8:33-34).

Rather than condemnation, there is now reconciliation.[25] The estrangement has been repaired; the alienation is over. Now there is again a relationship of intimacy and love, in which we as God's children are the recipients of his mercy and grace forever and ever. Never again can we be separated from God's love for us.

> Who shall separate us from the love of Christ? Shall trouble or hardship or persecution or famine or nakedness or danger or sword? . . . No, in all these things, we are more than conquerors through him who loved us. For I am convinced that neither death nor life, neither angels nor demons, neither the present nor the future, nor any powers, neither height nor depth, nor anything else in all creation, will be able to separate us from the love of God that is in Christ Jesus our Lord. (Rom 8:35, 37-39)

Experiencing God's peace. This peace and joy were experienced by Jesus' disciples after his resurrection. None of them had done well during the time of their Master's greatest need. When he was arrested in the Garden of Gethsemane, all of them had fled in fear (Mk 14:50).[26] While we naturally focus our primary attention on the betrayal of Judas and the denials of Peter, it was not the finest hour for any of Jesus' disciples. So when they gathered together on the first day of the week (three days after Jesus' death), they were experiencing, no doubt, a jumble of emotions. They remained fearful of the Jewish authorities, so much so that they met behind locked doors. There was a wild sense of hope in their hearts owing to the reports of Peter and John, who earlier that morning had seen Jesus' empty tomb. But this excitement was dampened by the burden of their guilt. Even if Jesus were somehow alive, surely he would be angry with them. After all, they had fallen away. They had failed their Lord precisely when he had needed their support the most. Such were their emotions when Jesus came into their locked room. John recorded the scene.

> On the evening of that first day of the week, when the disciples were together, with the doors locked for fear of the Jewish authorities, Jesus came and stood among them and said, "Peace be with you!" After he said this, he showed them his hands and side. The disciples were overjoyed when they saw the Lord. Again Jesus said, "Peace be with you! As the Father has sent me, I am sending you." And with that he breathed on them and said, "Receive the Holy Spirit." (Jn 20:19-22)

When Jesus came to this fearful, guilt-ridden group of his followers, he came bearing gifts. First and foremost was the gift of peace. Rather than being angry with his frail disciples, who had in fact failed him, Jesus twice offered them his peace. No hostility, no ongoing estrangement. Jesus came in peace, bringing to his disciples the gift of a fully restored, fully intimate and loving relationship with him.

It is important to note what occurred between the two times Jesus said, "Peace be with you." "After he had said this, he showed them his hands and his side" (Jn 20:20). Jesus' hands and side bore the scars of his suffering and death. His hands had been pierced with the nails. His side had been jabbed through with the sword of a Roman soldier while he was on the cross. Jesus' point, I believe, was that the peace he was offering to his disciples was a costly peace. Not costly to these disciples—no, it was a free gift of grace to them. But this peace was supremely costly to Jesus. It cost him his life.

But out of love for his heavenly Father and for his people, Jesus gladly paid that price. And then he came with peace, the kind of peace that made his disciples "overjoyed" (Jn 20:20).

But Jesus came with other gifts as well. Once reconciled to him, once embraced by his acceptance and love, these disciples were free to follow Jesus in his ongoing mission to the world. "As the Father has sent me, I am sending you," Jesus said (Jn 20:21). And to equip them for their mission, he breathed on them and said, "Receive the Holy Spirit" (Jn 20:22).

Peace and joy and mission; a renewed, reconciled relationship and a call to service—these are all gifts that come from the justifying grace of God through the death and resurrection of Jesus Christ. Jesus' disciples received those gifts. And so can you and I.

Forgiveness for those who have failed. When Jesus encountered his disciples after the resurrection, they were grappling with experiences of real and perceived failure. Consider the case of Thomas. He was not with the other disciples when Jesus met with them on that first Easter Sunday afternoon. When he heard the others tell him of being with Jesus, he was not at all convinced that they really had. Thomas demanded proof: "Unless I see the nail marks in his hands and put my finger where the nails were, and put my hand into his side, I will not believe" (Jn 20:25).

Christians of later generations have understood Thomas's response to be an occasion of doubt, so much so that we often identify him as "Doubting Thomas." Many have seen this as a failure of faith on the part of Thomas. I disagree. I'm not at all convinced that Thomas was doubting. He was, rather, seeking sufficient ground for his faith and was not willing to believe until he found it. I'm even surer that his experience was not a failure in any objective sense of the word (note the lack of rebuke from Jesus when he met with Thomas). But I suspect that when Thomas met Jesus, one week after the resurrection, he was struggling with a subjective feeling of failure. He had not believed when the other disciples had.

When Jesus met Thomas, his first words were exactly the same as his initial greeting to the others: "Peace be with you!" (Jn 20:26). To one struggling with his faith, Jesus came with the gift of peace. This gift is more than adequate to deal with the faith struggles of Thomas or any of his other followers or would-be followers. Jesus kindly offered Thomas his hands and his side to provide him with the evidence he needed. But the text never records Thomas putting his finger in the nail marks or his hand in his side. The presence of the risen Christ was more than enough for him to believe and to worship (Jn 20:28). Jesus' response was not one of rebuke, but rather of blessing (Jn 20:29).

But if Thomas's struggles were with perceived failure, how much deeper and more intense must the struggles have been within Peter's mind and heart. To be sure, Peter had been with the others on that first Easter Sunday and had heard Jesus' words of peace and mission. But could they really apply to him? After all, he had failed Jesus grievously—and sinfully. After boasting of his superior faithfulness and courage ("Even if all fall away on account of you, I never will," Mt 26:33), Peter had denied his Lord— not once but three times. In the midst of his third and most sordid denial, in which he called down curses on himself and swore that he didn't know Jesus (Mt 26:72), Jesus had looked at him, and his gaze had penetrated Peter's soul. Peter wept bitterly in response, but his tears could never erase the memory of that horrible night. The sound of the cock crowing and the smell of the charcoal fire were indelibly imprinted on him. How many times had Peter replayed the tapes in his mind? He could never undo what he had done. So the questions weighed heavily on him. How could Jesus possibly make peace with him? How could Jesus ever use him to further his mission?

This was the background of a dramatic encounter that the risen Christ had with Peter and five of the other disciples early one morning by the Sea of Galilee.[27] After having breakfast, Jesus turned his attention to Peter, saying, "Simon, son of John, do you love me more than these?" To hear Jesus refer to him as "Simon," his name before Jesus had renamed him Peter (the Rock), must have cut him to the heart. The form of Jesus' question was clearly designed to remind Peter of his false bravado and his misplaced boasting. With the smell of yet another charcoal fire in his nostrils, Peter was forced to confront his failure—and the lack of love behind it. His response was clear but probably tinged with sorrow and regret: "Yes, Lord, you know that I love you." Jesus replied, "Feed my lambs" (Jn 21:15).

Two other times, Jesus asked Peter about his love for him— clearly identifying the highest priority for Peter or any of his other followers. Both times, Peter responded affirmatively. And two times Jesus responded, not with anger, not with condemnation, but with acceptance and with a mission for his beloved Peter: "Take care of my sheep" and "Feed my sheep" (Jn 21:16-17).

In this encounter, Jesus asked Peter three questions (the number clearly corresponding to Peter's three denials). Peter responded with three confessions of his love for Jesus, and Jesus graciously commissioned him three times. What grace! What love! Jesus was making it abundantly clear that Peter's failure, grievous as it was, would not have the last word. It would not define Peter's identity for the rest of his life. It had not destroyed Jesus' relationship with him. No, Jesus' heart was filled with love for his frail and sometimes faltering Rock. There was forgiveness for Peter from the grace of God. There was a mission for him. And there is for us as well.

God continues to give his forgiveness and his mission to his children. Jeremy was a pre-med student preparing for medical school when his girlfriend became pregnant. He was not a follower of Christ, and while he felt some ambivalence about the issue of abortion, he didn't have the sense of right and wrong that would prohibit such an act. So in the crisis of an unplanned and unwanted pregnancy, Jeremy pressured his girlfriend to have an abortion.

It was some ten years later that Jeremy began to believe that he had "deeply violated the universe in a way that was somehow permanent and unfixable." The guilt he experienced for this act and the subsequent end of the relationship with his girlfriend contributed to an existential crisis that led Jeremy to "a deep search for meaning, purpose, value and truth." In the grace of God, this search ultimately led him to faith in Christ.

Through faith, Jeremy experienced forgiveness for all his sins, even this one. Part of the reason he is now so passionate about his faith, he says, is that only Christ can offer the forgiveness he needed so desperately. This forgiveness is a crucial part of what has motivated and empowered Jeremy to give himself to a medical practice that serves the needs of the poor and disenfranchised. Such is the power of forgiveness.

To be sure, there were other people who also experienced pain and loss as a result of Jeremy's decisions. His ex-girlfriend had to cope with grief, pain and loss, and with the knowledge that she was pressured into the decision to have an abortion. While I do not know the specifics of her ongoing story, I do know that the grace of God is available to her. And that their unborn child is in the hands of our loving heavenly Father. Even in the aftermath of such a tragedy, the grace of God is abundant to forgive and restore, to bring healing and hope.

This is the good news of Scripture for us in our sinful failures. All of them—past, present and future—have been forgiven by God through Christ.

6

More Truths of Grace

☞

Scripture has more good news for us as we grapple with the experience of failure. In this chapter, we will look at three more truths of grace. As with those considered in the previous chapter, these are grace-filled promises from God to every one of his children in Christ. And they are invitations of hope to all who are considering following him.

Truth of Grace 3: God Is Progressively Working to Transform Us and Our Sinful Failures

The good news is that God has acted graciously and decisively in Christ to deal with sin. As we have seen in the preceding chapter, God forgives us through the death and resurrection of Jesus. But he promises to do even more. By the power of his Spirit, God works to remove sin from the experience of his children. He works to cleanse us and purify us and transform us so that we can become more and more like Christ in our values, decisions and actions. All of this is what the apostle John meant when he said that Jesus Christ "appeared so that he might take away our sins" (1 Jn 3:5).[1]

Sanctification of the children of God. The traditional term that

Christians have used for this process of transformation is *sanctification*. The biblical words for it are related to the concept of holiness, which in turn is related to the concept of separateness or difference. What is holy is different from everything else. Supremely, this is true of God himself. He is absolutely unique— separate from and superior to everyone and everything else in the universe. But holiness is to characterize our lives as God's children as well. We, too, are to be different people and to live different lives because we belong to him.[2] Theologian J. I. Packer summarized this connection, saying, "Having at its root the thought of separation or apartness, [holiness] signifies, first, all that marks out God as set apart from [humans] and, second, all that should mark out Christians as set apart for God."[3] In our own experience, holiness is the living out of the values and the character of Jesus day by day.[4]

At the beginning of our Christian lives, God set us apart as belonging to him, and in this sense, all Christians are "holy."[5] But as we walk through life, we experience sanctification as a process. We are in a process of growth as God is progressively transforming us by his grace. As a result, Paul said that we "are being transformed into [Christ's] image with ever-increasing glory" and so "inwardly we are being renewed day by day" (2 Cor 3:18; 4:16).[6]

The testimony of Scripture is that this process of transformation is a lifelong one. The positive implication of this truth is that our whole lives as Christians can, and should, be a process of growth. This is the exciting "normal" for every Christian, as long as we live. But the other side is also true. None of us will ever arrive at a state of complete Christlikeness in this life. No matter how much progress we make, no matter how much growth we experience, we will always be struggling with sin this side of heaven.[7] Jesus instructed us in the Lord's Prayer to pray for the forgiveness of our sins (Mt 6:12). This prayer is just as much a daily necessity as is the request for daily bread that precedes it. We will never outgrow our battle against sin or our need of forgiveness for it. John tells us that "if we claim to be without sin, we deceive ourselves and the truth is not in us" (1 Jn 1:8). These words apply throughout our lives.[8]

Adjusting our expectations. The truth of progressive, lifelong sanctification contains good news for us as we continue to grapple with the reality of failure in our lives. It can help us adjust our expectations.

The New Testament vision of the Christian life is a hopeful one. While there remains a lifelong struggle against sin that all followers of Christ are engaged in, the reality is that God is at work to change us. We should expect growth and work toward it. The God who calls us to high standards of holiness[9] is the same God who lives in us by his Spirit and empowers us to say no to sin and to pursue the virtues of a Christlike character and life.[10] The fact that God himself is at work in us can encourage us and motivate us to press on and not give up in our pursuit of growth and transformation.

Paul commanded the Philippian believers to "continue to work out your salvation with fear and trembling" (Phil 2:12). This was a strong and stirring call to live out, in personal and corporate ways, the implications of God's saving work in their lives. Paul then went on to give the reason such moral effort is possible and productive: "For it is God who works in you to will and to act in order to fulfill his good purpose."[11] It is the inward working of God—at the level of willing and desiring as well as the level of action—that alone can give the Philippians—and us—the encouragement to continue to press on.

The apostle John made the same connection. He spoke of the ultimate goal of God's moral transformation in our lives—that when Christ appears, we shall be like him fully and completely, for "we shall see him as he is" (1 Jn 3:2). Then he wrote, "All those who have this hope in him purify themselves, just as he is pure." It is the sure hope of the completion of the process of transformation that encourages us and motivates us to keep on participating right now in the ongoing process of growth.

All of this is to say that there is no room for a despairing pessimism in the Christian life, a mindset and expectation that everything will stay the same and that our same struggles will continue to haunt us throughout our lives. The grace and power of God is more than sufficient to bring about the transformation we need and desire. So there is great reason for hope—not because of us, but because of the gracious commitment of our God to progressively change us and make us new. And because of this confident hope, we can and we must give ourselves to the process of growth.[12]

At the same time, however, we need to make sure that our expectations of growth and moral transformation are not unrealistically optimistic. If the moral transformation we need and long for is a lifelong process, we ought not be surprised that we continue to struggle with sin. While we do not want to excuse disobedience to God's will or to downplay the resources of his grace to empower us to resist temptations,[13] there is a certain inevitability to our failures in the ongoing struggle with sin.[14] Recognizing this fact and adjusting our expectations accordingly may be one of the single most important things we can do to help us cope well with our sinful failures.

It is natural for us as Christians to want to be like our heavenly Father. We want to be obedient to him and to live out his love and grace. We value growth and "victories" over temptation and sin. We readily want to share stories about triumphing over past struggles. We're eager to share our present state of joyful obedience (at least that's what we want to say about ourselves). As a result, we find that our communities are all too often places where we read-

ily share our successes and rarely, if ever, share our failures.
Consciously or subconsciously, many of us think that because
we love God and are genuinely seeking to be faithful to him, he
should enable us to gain total, complete and ongoing victory over
all sin—now and for the rest of our lives. That's how it's supposed
to be, isn't it?

If anything, this expectation is heightened for Christian leaders. My experience as a pastor and professor bears this out. I realize that many people have, at different times and in various ways,
put me on a pedestal due to my position of leadership. They have
high expectations of me (some of which are proper, but some of
which go beyond anything appropriate). Far more problematic,
however, is that I have all too often internalized these heightened
expectations. My expectations of myself not only include excel-
lence in my professional and ministerial duties, but also high levels of godly living. While at a theological level I disavow any claim
to "perfectionism" (the belief that we can achieve sinless perfection in this life), at a subjective and emotional level I can come
very close to expecting that of myself. I expect not to sin, and I
expect not to fail in other areas. I don't think I'm alone in this.

But it is precisely these expectations that make it all the more
devastating when reality confronts us. We find ourselves continuing to struggle. We disobey God. We experience other nonsinful failures as well. As a result, we not only experience guilt
and remorse over our sinful failures, we also experience a sense
of shame because we are not living up to our own expectations.
And we aren't living up to the successes we hear articulated by
others. So we shrink back, put on a plastic smile in our times
with one another and hide our true selves in silence. We feel
shamed into isolation and inauthenticity. And our silence hinders
us from making the progress and growth that God would want us
to make.

But why should we be surprised that we continue to struggle with sin when God has told us that our progressive sanctification will be a lifelong experience? How different our experience would be if we accepted this reality and let it free us to be honest about the struggles and failures we are currently experiencing. In honest sharing, in freely confessing our sins to one another, we can find strength in God and in our sisters and brothers to help us cope well and keep on making progress.

This is regularly the experience in Alcoholics Anonymous and other twelve-step recovery groups. The expectation is that everyone who attends an AA meeting does so out of need.[15] Attenders are alcoholics and affirm that in every meeting. Honest sharing is the norm, and there is freedom and transparency because everyone is being open and real. Acceptance in the midst of struggle is a given, because everyone is in the midst of the same struggle. Many recovering alcoholics say that such honesty, acceptance and genuine support make all the difference in their ongoing battle for sobriety.[16]

It is a stinging indictment of the church of Jesus Christ that so often we don't come close to these kinds of honest and open relationships. Theologically, we all affirm that we are sinners. We believe that we must acknowledge and confess our sins to receive forgiveness and enter into a new and transforming relationship with Jesus Christ. But somehow we have come to believe that our struggles with sin should stop there. We "have been saved," and so now we should be holy. Or at least we have to look that way to others. And so the cycle of shame and struggle continues.

In the seminary where I teach, I regularly have discussions with my students about why Christian leaders struggle morally and ethically in their lives and ministries. Why is it that some Christian leaders are leading double lives—whether it be in areas of sexual morality, family life, finances or other areas? We begin with the obvious (though too often overlooked) fact that Christian leaders are human beings like everyone else. Nothing in their calling from God or the positions they occupy endows them with an inherently higher degree of godliness. But there are some other unique factors that put Christian leaders at risk. They include the relational isolation that so many leaders experience. Also included are structural issues relating to employment and effectiveness in ministry: If I am really honest about my struggles with sin, will I get fired? Will others be willing and able to follow my leadership? High on the list is the heightened expectation levels we have for ourselves and think our significant others have for us as well. Tragically, we allow these internalized expectations to shame us into silence when we bump up against the reality of our ongoing and incomplete sanctification. Such silence gives new strength to the temptations we face. The end result can often be far more tragic and painful than might have been otherwise.

The good news of progressive sanctification. If our minds are truly renewed by the truth of progressive sanctification, we can relax. We can throw off the pressure to be perfect. Not only is this pressure stifling and burdensome, it is actually counterproductive. Our self-inflicted pressure to be perfect tends to focus our attention on ourselves and on our efforts to live the way God would want. But this egocentric self-focus is at the heart of the very sin we are trying to resist.

In the Middle Ages, theologians described our bent toward sin as being "curved in on ourselves."[17] Making progress in our struggle with this bent toward self-centeredness will not come from a heightened pressure to be perfect. Rather, throwing off such expectations can set us free to look away from ourselves and to look to God and the power of his Spirit to continue the process of moral transformation in our lives. It may seem paradoxical, but recognizing that we will never be totally free from sin in this life is actually one of the most significant steps we can take toward our own growth in Christlikeness.

Author Jean Blomquist described a surprising lesson she has learned from reflecting on failure in her life.

Failure can be a relief. When I could honestly admit—without denigrating myself—that I could never be perfect, I could finally get off my own back. In doing so, I became freer to use and explore the gifts God gave me. I became more accepting of my work and more willing to try new things. . . . I became less judgmental, more compassionate, more encouraging. Other's weaknesses were no longer indictments of my own weaknesses but possible places for healing, cooperation, and growth.[18]

Freedom, relief and hope really do come from genuinely accepting ourselves and the inevitable struggles with sin that we all experience. No doubt, it is humbling to admit that as long as we live we will continue to struggle and we will never fully and finally master sin until we see the Lord face to face (1 Jn 3:2). But there is much grace in humility. And there is much joy as well. By taking the pressure of perfection off our shoulders, the truth can set us free to keep on growing and to make progress in living and loving as Christ would in the world.

Such is the paradoxical complexity of our lives in Christ. Confidence in the power of God to bring about transformation in our lives and patience with ourselves in the midst of the lifelong process; honesty with God and others about the struggles we face; and a deep, heartfelt trust in the wisdom of God in guiding how far and how fast the transformation will take place—all are part and parcel of living as a follower of Christ. All are a part of God's gracious gift of transformation.

Truth of Grace 4: No Failure Defines
Our Identity as Christians

While our struggle with sin is indeed a lifelong process, as followers of Christ we engage in that struggle from the reality of a new identity. The New Testament heralds this good news: in Jesus Christ, we have been adopted as God's beloved daughters and sons. Not only does God the Judge declare that those who trust in Christ are forgiven and righteous before him, but God the Father embraces us in his love and adopts us into his beloved family forever. It is this gracious gift of adoption, and the relationship of love and intimacy it brings about, that should define our identity rather than any failure or collection of failures, or conversely, any success or collection of successes.

Adoption: A relationship of love and joy. The New Testament speaks of our adoption as being conceived in God's love before the creation of the earth: "In love, [God] predestined us for adoption to sonship through Jesus Christ, in accordance with his pleasure and will" (Eph 1:5).[19] And our status as children of God and the resulting relationship is an overflowing expression of the abundance of God's love. "See what great love the Father has lavished on us, that we should be called the children of God" (1 Jn 3:1).

J. I. Packer rightly noted that "closeness, affection, and generosity are at the heart of this [family] relationship." He concluded, "To be right with God the judge is a great thing, but to be loved and cared for by God the father is even greater."[20]

Not only is our experience as adopted children of God one of love, it is also one of joy. It is in our secure status as beloved children of God that we can "rejoice in the Lord always" (Phil 4:4). Knowing that we are eternally loved by our heavenly Father can free us to respond in love to him and to others. And according to Jesus, this is the pathway to joy—that his joy might be in us and our joy might be full (Jn 15:11).

But we are not the only ones to experience joy. Our heavenly Father rejoices in every one of his children and in the family relationship he has established. The prophet Zephaniah speaks very powerfully about this joy of God: "The LORD your God is with you, the Mighty Warrior who saves; he will take great delight in you; in his love he will no longer rebuke you, but will rejoice over you with singing" (Zeph 3:17). Imagine the reality that the God of the universe, our heavenly Father, rejoices over us with singing! Such is the reality for all whom God adopts into his family.

A loving father? For many in our world today, however, this concept of God as a loving and joyful father seems impossible to believe. For them, it is virtually inconceivable, because their relationships with their own fathers have been anything but good. Many grow up in single-parent families with no father. Others find that their fathers, while physically present, are emotionally absent. Far too many other children, rather than experiencing affirmation, affection and safety in a loving relationship with their father, experience an abusive relationship instead—involving physical, emotional, verbal and/or sexual abuse. In other contexts, the issues are far less severe, but the deficiencies are nonetheless very real. As a result, our responses to the biblical proclamation that God is a loving heavenly Father to all his children in Christ can range from flat-out rejection (if God is a father, I don't want anything to do with him), to suspicion, to uncertainty.

But even in the worst cases, I believe there is good news in the reality of our adoption. Let me suggest two ways we can approach this relationship.

First, we can, and we must, form our concept of God as a loving father in contrast to as well as in comparison with our earthly fathers. Even those who have had horrific relationships with their fathers often have an instinctive sense of what a good father should be. In the same way that married couples often seek a relationship with each other that is different from and superior to what they have experienced in their own families of origin, it is possible for Christians to understand a relationship with their heavenly Father that is different from and superior to anything they have experienced with their earthly fathers.[21] There is a wide spectrum, to be sure, based on the varieties of relationships we have with our earthly fathers, but from Scripture and from our experience in relationship with God, we can all find ourselves saying, "In some ways God is just like my father, only more so!" and "In other ways, he is not at all like my father."[22]

Second, and even more helpful, is the fact that God has not left us in the dark as to what it means for him to be a father. He does not want us to be in the position where all we can do is draw analogies from our earthly fathers. He has revealed to us the depth of his fatherly love in his relationship with his Son, Jesus Christ.[23] And in turn, Jesus reveals to us what it means to relate to God as a father.

The Gospel of John is a valuable resource for us in this. It describes God as relating to Jesus, his Son, through guidance and direction (which Jesus delights to follow),[24] through love and affection,[25] through closeness and intimacy,[26] and through the honor the Father purposes to shower on his Son.[27] But perhaps the richest portrait of God as our Father comes in the Gospel of Luke.

A father who loves. "There was a man who had two sons." With these simple words, Jesus began perhaps his most well-known parable, found in Luke 15:11-32. We often refer to it as the parable of the prodigal son.[28] But that name hardly does justice to the parable, for both sons of the father are central characters in the parable, and even more important, Jesus' primary focus is on the father himself.[29]

In the parable, the father shows his amazing love for his younger son—who asked him for his share of the inheritance (in first-century Palestinian culture this was tantamount to wishing him dead),[30] who went to a distant country and who "squandered his wealth in wild living" (Lk 15:13). When his money ran out and he began to starve, this son decided to go home. He rehearsed a statement of repentance and apology, and set off.

When the son was still a long way away, his father saw him coming home (I suspect he was watching for him) and, in an act utterly foreign to a wealthy, middle-aged, Jewish man, ran to him. Filled with compassion, he threw his arms around him and kissed him. He cut short his son's confession and had the best robe, ring and sandals brought to him. And he ordered his servants to prepare a feast to celebrate this marvelous homecoming: "Bring the fattened calf and kill it. Let's have a feast and celebrate. For this son of mine was dead and is alive again; he was lost and is found" (Lk 15:23-24).

The father had an elder son, with whom he was no less loving. This son had never left home; he had worked for his father his whole life. But his anger over the celebration for his brother revealed that his heart was indeed far from his father. But even when he refused to come into the feast, the father did not neglect him. He went out and pleaded with his older son, assuring him of his love and of the fact that he was and always would be his son. "My son, you are always with me, and everything I have is yours. But we had to celebrate and be glad, because this brother of yours was dead and is alive again; he was lost and is found" (Lk 15:31-32).

The father's love for his younger, wayward son was expressed in his lavish welcome, based not on his son's actions but solely on his own grace and mercy. The love of the father for his older son, who was physically close to home but far away in heart, was expressed in an invitation—an invitation to join in and experience the joy and forgiveness and intimacy of grace. This expression of love was different from what he gave his elder son, but it is love

nonetheless. Both expressions of love show us the heart of the
Father who adopts us through Jesus Christ.

Living as beloved children. When we live out of the love of our
heavenly Father and out of our identity as his beloved children,
this profoundly impacts us. New York City pastor Tim Keller has
recently noted that, among people who profess faith in Christ,
there are two fundamentally different narrative identities that
dominate our lives.

The first he calls the moral-performance narrative identity.
This is the identity of those who, in their heart of hearts, understand their lives in terms of the principle "I obey; therefore I am
accepted by God." The second Keller calls the grace narrative
identity. This identity is shaped by the heart conviction that "I am
accepted by God through Christ; therefore I obey."[31]

Keller suggests that people living out of each narrative identity
may do many of the same activities. They may seek to love God
and their neighbors, to be good family members and work associates, to pray, to worship, to give generously, and so on. But according to Keller, "They are doing so out of radically different motives,
in radically different spirits, resulting in radically different personal characters."

For those who live out of the moral-performance identity, issues
of success and failure are crucial. Their success—whether in cultural terms of wealth, power and prestige or in religious terms, such
as being a good person and obeying God—is what determines their
identity and their significance. This makes failures of any kind devastating. When these people are criticized, their entire self-image is
under attack, and the experience can be devastating. They tend to
respond either by crumbling under the weight of guilt and shame or
by angrily and self-righteously attacking their critics. In the end,
this unhealthy and distorted sense of identity tends to manifest itself in many of the very kinds of failure they fear so much.

On the other hand, those who live out of the grace identity understand at emotional as well as cognitive levels that their identity is not determined by their successes or their failures. As children of God, they are not loved more by their Father because of their successes, nor are they loved less as a result of their failures. Their significance is not determined by their success. This provides them with the emotional ballast to weather criticism and to respond humbly and gratefully to both their successes and their failures.

The freedom and power for God-honoring living that comes from accepting and internalizing our identity as those who are accepted and loved children of God in Christ is very great. We can see this in the experience of Jan.

Jan was raised in the church, yet she describes her faith as being clearly of the moral-performance variety, especially in her teen years. Throughout her life, she has struggled with melancholy, anxiety, apathy and guilt. After the death of her grandmother, these emotions caused her to question her own relationship with God. She recalls being overwhelmed with worry that she would not receive salvation at the end of her life. After all, how could her faith be good enough if she was sad, anxious and felt guilty?

Jan's high school years were a roller coaster of good intentions (to be kind at school, patient with others, a "good witness" and so on) and feelings that she was always falling short. Given her performance-based faith, these experiences left her constantly feeling guilty.

In college, things worsened. During those years, Jan started to doubt and to question her faith for the first time. Things that had seemed so black-and-white before now appeared to be murky and gray. This was a frightening experience for Jan. "I felt like my questioning and doubting was a sin. For the first time I felt isolated and detached from God." Her friends were concerned for her as well and sought to give to her a "quick spiritual fix," rather than trusting Jan and God's work in her as she "walked into the gray."

As the years went by, Jan's questioning continued, and she felt she was hanging on to her faith by a thread. But a new faith community made a huge difference for her. She started to learn about the love of God her Father, a love based on his grace and not on her performance. All along she had never felt she was good enough to deserve God's love, but she was beginning to experience the father heart of God. She recalls a mentor telling her that God doesn't have expectations for his children, only anticipations. She was greatly helped by friends who showed her how to internalize the realities of grace and to let go of the guilt she had been carrying. It was on a short-term mission trip to Africa that this new view of God crystallized in her mind and heart.

Jan would be the first to admit that her journey with God is in process and that progress is incremental. Her questions continue, as do her disappointments. But she is very hopeful as she speaks of a new and more authentic relationship with God in the midst of her wrestling.

> I have come to embrace the questions and wrestling because I see it brings me to a deeper, more intimate relationship with God. I thank God for my failure to not completely understand his character. My years of melancholy, anxiety, apathy, discontentment and guilt have brought me to my own authentic relationship with him. I am filled with peace through my searching because he has taught me that he welcomes it and is walking with me through it.

Truth of Grace 5: No Failure Will Have the Last Word in Our Lives

Without doubt, our experiences of failure are painful. At times, they are shattering, and we are tempted to define our lives and ourselves by them. We can so identify with a failed marriage, the bankruptcy of the family business or the ways our children have turned out that don't fit our expectations that we begin to wonder if this is the final word.

But Scripture triumphantly proclaims a different outcome. No failure—no matter how serious, no matter how devastating to us and to our loved ones, no matter how open and public—will have the last word. The Bible is insistent: God will triumph in the end. And that means his grace will always have the last word in our lives.

Our ultimate hope. The final scene of the last book of the Bible paints the picture of a "new heaven and new earth" that God is creating as the eternal home for all his children. The portrait is breathtaking. As he saw this new heaven and new earth, John, the writer of the book of Revelation, heard a loud voice coming from the throne of God:

> Look! God's dwelling place is now among the people, and he will dwell with them. They will be his people, and God himself will be with them and be their God. "He will wipe every tear from their eyes. There will be no more death" or mourning or crying or pain, for the old order of things has passed away. (Rev 21:3-4)

Here is the fullness of all of God's saving mercy: no more death or mourning or crying or pain. At this point, failure will be a thing of the past, and its sting will be wiped from our consciousness forever. God will fully and forever redeem all our failures—sinful and nonsinful. He will heal our hurts and dry our tears. God himself will be with us and will fill us completely with joy and peace and love forever.

Redeeming our failures. The amazing thing is that God will actually use all our failures to help bring this about. Scripture proclaims that all the pain and hardship in our lives (including all that comes from the failures we have experienced) is used redemptively by God in his creation of the new heaven and new earth. This is perhaps stated most clearly in 2 Corinthians 4:17: "For our light and momentary troubles are achieving for us an eternal glory that outweighs them all."

Paul's words are shocking. He described his own troubles and sufferings and those of his readers as being "light and momentary." If he were not one who knew the reality and depth of suffering in his own life, we might well think of him as being insensitive and naïve about the realities of life (see 2 Cor 11:23-29 for Paul's description of his sufferings). But he was not. Rather, Paul was intentionally taking the long view, the eternal perspective. He affirmed that all human suffering, no matter how long it might last and no matter how intense it might be, is actually "light and momentary" in comparison with the eternal glory and joy that God is preparing for his children. So great, so deep, so long-lasting is this joy that it makes even the worst of our sufferings pale in comparison.

Perhaps the most hopeful part of Paul's statement is that by the grace of God our troubles and sufferings are actually "achieving" the eternal joy God is preparing for his children.[32] Our pain is not unproductive. We do not suffer in vain. This in no way justifies our sinful failures or the sin that others commit against us. They remain sinful and opposed to God's purposes and intentions. But the good news is, in the mystery of redeeming grace, God actually uses all our suffering to produce his final triumph. Far from ultimately and finally devastating us, our failures and the pain we experience as a result are actually the building blocks of the joy, love and peace that we can experience throughout our lives and for all eternity.

It is impossible for us to go back in time and redo the past, such that our failures never existed. But the good news is that God redeems them and transforms them and uses them for our eternal joy.

Lessons we learn. Sometimes this transformation comes from lessons we learn as we grapple with failure. J. K. Rowling eloquently testified to this in her 2008 commencement address at Harvard University. She spoke of what she called "the fringe benefits of failure." She recounted a time in her life, seven years after her own graduation from university, when by any conventional measurement she had failed "on an epic scale." Her marriage had imploded; she was a single parent; and by her own testimony, she was "as poor as it is possible to be in modern Britain, without being homeless." It was a very dark time in her life. But, according to Rowling, it was not without its benefits. Her failure stripped away what was inessential in her life and forced her to stop pretending she was anything other than who she was. This in turn gave her the freedom to focus her energies on the only work that really mattered to her. Rowling's reflections are worth quoting at length.

> I was set free, because my greatest fear had been realised, and I was still alive, and I still had a daughter whom I adored, and I had an old typewriter and a big idea. And so rock bottom became the solid foundation on which I rebuilt my life. . . . Failure gave me an inner security that I had never attained by passing examinations. Failure taught me things about myself that I could have learned no other way. I discovered that I had a strong will, and more discipline than I had suspected; I also found out that I had friends whose value was truly above the price of rubies. The knowledge that you have emerged wiser and stronger from setbacks means that you are, ever after, secure in your ability to survive. You will never truly know yourself, or the strength of your relationships, until both have been tested by adversity. Such knowledge is a true gift, for all that it is painfully won,

and it has been worth more than any qualification I ever
earned. . . . Life is difficult, and complicated, and beyond
anyone's total control, and the humility to know that will
enable you to survive its vicissitudes.[33]

Jean Blomquist also affirms the potential for us to learn from
our failures: "Failure, for all its harshness and darkness, may lead
us to the light. This is the time when, because of our neediness
and poverty, we are often most open and receptive to the movement of the Spirit."[34] Many of the men and women whose stories I
have shared in earlier chapters testify to this reality.

Often the light we receive from God through our failures comes
in the form of a greater and more accurate self-knowledge. Samantha says that in and through the trauma of her two marriages, she
learned both how strong and how weak she could be, all at the
same time. Navigating the ending of her engagement due to her
fiancé's infidelity has helped Lori grow in her ability to distinguish what is really her responsibility and what is not. She says
that she has learned "that I'm not perfect and can't control everything—especially not how other people feel and act; all I can do is
work on being the best me I can be. . . . Also I learned to take responsibility for my own actions, choices and circumstances and
not be a victim." As Sue continues to wrestle with the reality that
her daughter is not actively following Christ, she says she is increasingly able to realize that her daughter's decisions are out of
her hands. This helps her in the difficult process of letting go of
her feelings of responsibility for her daughter's actions.

Sometimes our failures teach us to recognize and appreciate
more fully our unique set of strengths and weaknesses. Barb has
grown in and through her vocational struggles to pay more attention "to what excites and energizes me." She has also been learning about how she functions best, specifically that "guilt is a lousy

motivator." The experience of being fired from two jobs not only helped Jim to identify some of his attitudes that needed to be changed, it also helped him evaluate his career path. Not only did it deepen his faith in God, it was a crucial part of the process leading him to graduate school.

In addition, experiences of failure can lead to reprioritizing what is truly important. John was a wrestler in college. He was a walk-on, having not been recruited out of high school. Yet through lots of hard work (as a walk-on, he always felt he needed to work twice as hard as the scholarship athletes), he made the team. Eventually he was awarded a scholarship, a greatly appreciated recognition of his ability and hard work from his coach.

But throughout four years of wrestling, John never became a regular starter. All his hard work notwithstanding, he never became, in his coach's words, "the big dog." To have failed to achieve this goal that he longed for and had worked so hard for felt humiliating. When the team would travel to an away match without him, he would try to stay in sick as much as possible—just so no one would ask why he wasn't with them.

This continued for four years of collegiate wrestling. As he was graduating, John stood before his teammates and spoke of what he had learned from his successes and failures on the mat. He told how he had learned that character and integrity are far more important than any amount of athletic success. No doubt, his wrestling career had more than its share of disappointments. But John said that he wouldn't have traded any of them, for without them, he wouldn't have become the person he is today. And that quality of person was recognized by his coaches as they voted him the most dedicated wrestler on the team.

Another lesson we can learn from our failures involves our understanding and experience of God. Samantha not only learned how weak and how strong she could be, but the failure of her marriages resulted in a very deep experience of God's love for her. Jim's loss of jobs was the occasion for him to experience the material provision of God in unusual and unexpected ways. "All in all, I wish that there had been an easier way to see God's faithfulness and provision, but it has been an amazing example of his love." Jennifer's failure to follow the usual college path of her family helped her to learn how God can transform and redeem a failure. "I learned it's okay to fail, because one person's failure can become their success." Perhaps the most important lesson of all, she says, is "to turn to God, instead of being angry at him for the failure. He knows exactly what he's doing, and all he does is good."[35]

Sometimes the lesson learned is that we don't know all the answers. Joy has gone through five years of infertility, and her pain was intensified by a miscarriage and an ectopic pregnancy. But through her pain she has grown. "I no longer believe that being a Christian means I have an answer, and I understand that answers don't really help anyway. I'm much better at sitting with someone during his or her painful times, because I like it when people do that with me." Her transformation has come in part from learning to trust in the healing grace of God. "I now know that I can find happiness in the midst of life circumstances I would previously have thought intolerable, and I trust that God heals my perspective and my expectations as well as my heart, so that I can bloom where I am planted."

But not every time does failure result in lessons that we are consciously aware of. Bill went through some significant and painful emotional struggles while studying overseas during his college years. Reflecting back on that difficult experience, he is not at all sure what he was supposed to learn through it all. Many times our experiences of struggle and pain are like Bill's. God is still at work, but he is operating at the deepest levels of our minds and hearts, often beyond our conscious awareness. The fact that we cannot see and identify his work does not mean that he is not active. The burden of Scripture is to tell us *that* he is at work, not necessarily *how* he is working. Other times, the work God is doing through our struggles and failures is primarily for the benefit of other people. And we may not yet be able to see what he is doing in their lives.

In the end, we will often have to journey with God in the darkness. He asks us to trust him and his grace—in the words of Paul, to "live by faith and not by sight" (2 Cor 5:7). But while the path is often murky and shrouded in mystery, the final destination is not. God has proclaimed to us our ultimate home, the new heavens and the new earth, where there will be "no more death or mourning or crying or pain."

This is our ultimate hope. And hope changes everything about our lives here and now, including the ways we seek to cope with our failures. It has been said that if a person has hope, he or she can endure almost anything. But without hope, even relatively small difficulties can be crushing burdens. Hope changes everything—provided that hope is sure.

A certain hope. During my years in seminary in New England, I became a fan of the Boston Celtics. They are a storied NBA franchise, who prior to our years in New England had won many championships under their legendary coach Red Auerbach. This Hall of Fame coach was well known for a particular element of his coaching style. Throughout the game, he was constantly on his feet, prowling the sidelines as he urged his team on to victory. But when he concluded that the game had reached a point where the outcome had been decided and a Celtics victory was assured, he would sit down on the bench and light a big cigar. This was his trademark signal that it was only a matter of time before the victory would be final.

Sometimes in a close game, Coach Auerbach would light his

victory cigar only very shortly before the final buzzer. But in other games, he would light that victory cigar much earlier. In those situations, the lit cigar did not end the game. No, there were more minutes to be played, more shots to be made, more rebounds to be gathered in. At times there were even injuries in those final minutes. But none of that would affect the outcome. The final minutes of those games were played with a confident expectation of final victory. The coach had signaled his sure and certain confidence of that.

The New Testament declares that we are living in a period analogous to the final minutes of a Boston Celtics victory. The ultimate victory of God over all the forces of sin and evil and death is sure. It was accomplished supremely through the life, death and resurrection of Christ. Because of Christ, we can be assured of the final outcome. This does not mean that we no longer struggle in life, that we no longer experience failure and the pain it brings to us and to those we love—any more than Red Auerbach's victory cigar automatically protected his players from errors or injury. But the victory won by Jesus Christ over all the powers of darkness guarantees our ultimate hope.[36] And this gives us the hope to press on.

This is good news! No failure will ever have the last word in our lives. God will ultimately triumph. The new heavens and new earth is coming. Our ultimate future will be filled with joy and with love. All our pain and suffering will be used redemptively by God to bring this about. And this sure and confident hope changes everything about the way we grapple with and walk through our experiences of failure.

7

Responding to Failure

❧

One eloquent statement of the central thesis of this book comes from John Gardner, professor of public service in the Graduate School of Business at Stanford University.

> Everyone fails. When Joe Louis was world heavyweight boxing champion, he said, "Everyone has to figure to get beat some time." The question isn't did you fail, but did you pick yourself up and move ahead.[1]

This is the crucial issue for each and every one of us—not *if* we will fail, but how we will respond when we *do* fail. This is the question we want to explore in more detail in this chapter.

Connecting the Head and the Heart

In the past two chapters, we have reviewed five very significant truths of grace from Scripture that can help us cope wisely and well with failure. We all need these truths. We need our minds to be renewed by them so we can respond to failure as God would have us respond.

But, as essential as right thinking is, it's not enough in and of itself. We need to do more than know these truths cognitively. We also need to internalize them and relate to them in emotional and volitional ways.[2] In other words, we need to connect our heads and our hearts.[3]

It has been said that the longest distance in the Christian life is the few inches that separate our heads from our hearts. All too often, we *know* these truths of grace, but we don't *feel* them. We don't embrace them (or perhaps more accurately, we don't allow them to embrace us). So our hearts remain unchanged, and we don't live out the truths of grace as we should.

The question before us is very simple: How can we traverse those crucial few inches that connect our heads and our hearts? There are no magic formulas or silver bullets that work infallibly on every occasion. But let me suggest several spiritual disciplines that can help.

Spiritual Disciplines

Spiritual disciplines are various human activities that God has characteristically been pleased to use to channel his grace into the lives of his people.[4] Dutch Catholic priest and writer Henri Nouwen affirmed that such spiritual practices "create some inner and outer space in our lives" that God uses to transform us so that we can live more and more like Jesus did.[5]

Dallas Willard, a noted writer on Christian spiritual formation, wrote, "We *can* become like Christ by doing one thing—by following him in the overall style of life he chose for himself. . . . We can, through faith and grace, become like Christ by arranging our whole lives around the activities he himself practiced in order to remain constantly at home in the fellowship of his Father." Describing this lifestyle, Willard said that Jesus "practiced such things as solitude and silence, prayer, simple and sacrificial living, intense study and meditation upon God's word and God's ways, and service to others."[6] These are practices that Willard calls spiritual disciplines.[7]

Spiritual director and professor Mary Darling argues that any human practice can become a means of grace if it is done intentionally, regularly over time and with the goal of becoming formed into Christlikeness.[8] We have already talked about some of these spiritual practices in earlier chapters of this book, such as confessing our sins to trusted friends and advisers (chapters four and six) and self-examination (especially in chapter five, in which we spoke of our need to grow in distinguishing between guilt and regret). Other disciplines such as journaling, silence, worship, celebration and service are critical as well. But in what follows, I would like to reflect on three crucial spiritual practices: meditation, prayer and honest involvement with others in community.

Meditation. Meditating on Scripture goes beyond reading or studying the Bible for information. Studying the truths of grace that we have been discussing is very important, but internalizing these truths involves more than that. It involves meditating on them. Meditation is an essential part of the process of turning our cognitive knowledge *about* God into relational and intimate knowledge *of* God.[9]

Bruce Demarest, a contemporary writer on Christian spirituality, says that meditation involves "giving *attention* with *intention*." As such, it involves "deep, repetitive reflection" on what God is saying.[10] In other words, meditation is a way of living in a text or a theme of Scripture, of soaking in it until its truth fills our minds, hearts and lives. As we do so, we ask God to use his word to change us at the depths of our being.[11] That is our intention, our goal.

To be sure, meditation involves our cognitive thinking processes. But it involves our imaginations as well. Let me suggest two ways that imagination can be involved in our meditation.

First, imagination can be directed *backward* in time as we seek to enter into a biblical narrative. Whether the text recounts Peter being forgiven and recommissioned by Jesus after the resurrection, Moses and the water God brought out of the rock in the desert, Jacob wresting with God and overcoming by being overcome, Jesus taking the towel and basin to serve his disciples by washing their feet or any other happening, we seek to live in the story. Through the use of holy creativity we immerse ourselves in it. We try to imagine all that went on—all the sights and sounds and smells. Only as we intentionally and imaginatively involve ourselves in the biblical narrative can we begin to see how it intersects with the narrative of our own life.

Second, we also look *forward*. Central to the process of meditating on Scripture is imagining a new future, a new reality that we would experience if we really believed and lived out this particular truth or text. Such holy and creative imagination creates a vision for what life could look like in response to what God is saying. What would be different about our relationships and our jobs; what would be different about the ways we respond to failure in these or any other area of our lives—if we could only embrace these truths of grace wholeheartedly? What might it look like, for example, if we were to embrace and live out our ultimate identity as beloved children of God rather than identifying so closely with our failures that we come to view ourselves as failures?

Envisioning such a new reality is often the first step of moving toward it, for we are drawn by what we see to be a desirable and valuable future. A compelling vision has great power to bring about what is foreseen. Walt Disney exemplified the power of such a vision. Soon after the completion of Disney World, someone said, "Isn't it too bad that Walt Disney didn't live to see this!" Mike Vance, creative director of Disney Studios replied, "He did see it—that's why it's here."[12]

Both uses of imagination—looking backward and looking forward—are important aspects of meditating on Scripture. And meditation is a key means of grace that God uses to connect our heads and our hearts.

A corollary to meditating on Scripture involves meditating on our own lives and experiences. When we fail, we need to look at our failure squarely and see what we can learn from it. Pastor and author Crawford Loritts has wisely said that "unexamined failure teaches you nothing."[13] Examining ourselves and our failures can help us see lessons God would have us learn—lessons about who we are and are not, lessons about what should be truly important in our lives, lessons about who God is and what he promises to do. Looking deeply at ourselves and our failures—alone in prayerful self-examination and together with trusted friends and advisers— is a valuable part of processing all our experiences.[14]

But it is important to keep in mind the reality we discussed in chapter six: we are not always consciously aware of the lessons. If our desire to look for lessons comes with the conscious or subconscious expectation that we will always be able to discern what they are, we can set ourselves up for frustrations God never intended for us. Yes, it is wise for us to examine ourselves and our failures. Yes, it is appropriate to ask God to show us whatever it is he would have us learn. But we need to bow humbly before a God who has never promised to reveal to us all the specifics of what he is doing. And we need to walk with him by faith and not by sight— through the light *and* the darkness.

In the final analysis, only God can change our hearts, and the good news is that he is eager to do so. In his love, God desires to transform his children so that they become more and more like Christ. This does not mean we will never fail again. But it does mean that, increasingly, we will respond wisely and well to the challenges that our failure brings.

Prayer. Our confidence in God as the one who changes us will be reflected in our asking him to do so. Prayer is a mutual dialogue we are privileged to have with God. Many of us think of prayer primarily or even exclusively as involving our requests, and it is important for us to bring our requests to God. Scripture invites us and commands us to do so, and our loving God promises that he will hear and respond to them.[15] This is true when we pray about our own needs. It is also true when others pray for us and when we pray for them. The power of a community united in prayer is very great.[16]

When Jan was on a short-term mission trip in Africa, others prayed that she would be able to understand God's love for her—in her heart and not just in her head. She describes the experience: "It was during that prayer that I realized I had never let God's love embrace me where I was." God answered her prayer and those of her community, and God's love has increasingly become a heart reality for her, and not just a theologically correct set of thoughts. This has enabled her to see God in a new, beautiful light and to enjoy a deeper, more intimate relationship with him.

But there is far more to the dialogue than our requests. In prayer, we also seek to listen to what God has to say to us, and perhaps most important of all, we seek to be in God's presence and to rest in his love. George MacDonald wrote, "Communion with God is the one need of the soul beyond all other needs; prayer is the beginning of that communion."[17] And it is this loving intimacy with God that transforms us and the failures of our lives.[18]

Brad and his wife are missionaries in an Eastern European country. Arriving there at the age of twenty-six, Brad finally felt he was doing the "job" he had always dreamed of. As with many young missionaries, he and his wife came with high hopes, dreams and expectations. But within six months, many of his hopes had been dashed. A mild depression started to form when he realized he had made a five-year commitment to this ministry and it was proceeding in very disappointing ways. Some of the unfulfilled expectations had to do with others around him, some with the inherent difficulties of the ministry. But at the deepest level, Brad struggled with himself. It seemed that his personality and skill sets were not adequate for the job.

The next two and a half years saw some slow progress. Life and ministry in this new country continued to be a daily struggle. Then a breakthrough came during a season of prayer out in the hills surrounding his country's capital city. As Brad told the Lord how much he felt like a failure and how sorry he was for not doing a better job, he sensed the Lord telling him, "You haven't failed. You've lived . . . and you will teach others with your experiences." Brad writes,

> When he said to me, "You've lived," the sense was that I have been human . . . just the way he designed me to be. I've lived as a human . . . as his creation . . . as he planned for me to live. The goal is not success in the sense that we humans think of it. The goal is being with him through the whole process of learning and life. As I walked with him through this process, he was pleased with me and affirmed me saying that I'm fully alive as he designed me to be. Oh, the freedom this brought me!

Along with that growing sense of freedom came a redefinition of success and hope for the future. "Success no longer meant doing the job I've been given (though of course I want to be a faithful worker), rather it was to live out life with Jesus, abide in him and let him determine the type of fruit that will come. If it looks different than I thought, that's okay." Intimate communion with Jesus throughout all the ups and downs of life was radically transforming for Brad.

Honest involvement with others in community. From the very beginning, God created human beings for relationships.[19] As noted earlier, God looked at all he had made and pronounced it "good," but after his creation of humans, he called it "very good." Prior to the entrance of sin into the world, there was only one thing God deemed to be "not good": "It is not good for the man to be alone" (Gen 2:18). And so God created the first woman to form a community and to meet the need for relationships.

Jesus himself said that the most important things in life involve relationships—loving God and loving our neighbors. And central to the kind of love God calls us to, both with himself and with one another, is truth.

Christians have long believed that God is a God of truth, not only in the truth he reveals to us but also in the truth he wants from us. God wants us to be honest with him about who we are, how we have lived, our successes and our failures.[20] And he longs for us to be honest with others. Truth and transparency are crucial.

The apostle John said, "If we walk in the light, as [God] is in the light, we have fellowship with one another, and the blood of Jesus, his Son, purifies us from all sin" (1 Jn 1:7). While much more is undoubtedly meant by that phrase, crucial to the concept of "walking in the light" is being open, honest and transparent. Such honest transparency with God is undoubtedly important. But since John was talking about having "fellowship with one another," he was also stressing openness and honesty in our relationships in community.

Bringing all of our lives into the light—the good, the bad and the ugly—is a vehicle for us to experience the cleansing, purifying grace of God in Christ. I repeat what I said already: not all failures are sinful. But if God promises that walking in the light can be a means of experiencing purification from sinful failures, just think of what it can do for the shame, anger and feelings of inadequacy that come from other kinds of failures.

When we walk in the light with others, they can in turn be honest with us. They can confront us and speak truth into our lives. Often this truth is easier to internalize when we hear it from others.

Not only can others speak truths from God into our minds and hearts, our friends themselves can be expressions of God's grace. All too often the shame we experience because of our failures makes us feel unacceptable to others.[21] But when others are present with us, when they express love and acceptance to us even in the midst of our failures, we can see and experience the love and acceptance of God. It is in the context of such mutual honesty and mutual love that we can follow God together.[22]

I've spoken of being in mutually honest, loving relationships with "one another." But who should those people be? All of us have had the stinging experience of trusting someone with deep information about us, only to have that person use it against us. Few things in life are as painful as this kind of betrayal. Wisdom is certainly called for in terms of whom to be open, honest and transparent with.

Many of the people who shared their stories of failure with me in preparation for writing this book commented on how counselors have been very helpful in this regard. Often the pain arising from failure is sufficiently intense and the issues involved are complex enough that those with special gifts, training and expertise are needed. (In chapter one, I shared about how valuable Jack Harrison, a fellow pastor and gifted counselor, was to Susan and me in our time of crisis.)

Other times, the people God uses to help us are spiritual directors or other spiritual helpers who are gifted in helping us listen to what God is doing in and through our failures.[23] On other occasions, those who have gone through similar experiences are invaluable.[24] And for still others, the needed help and support comes from family and close friends who can offer them prayer, encouragement and reminders of God's promises.

Sue shared how, in the pain and regret she and her husband felt over their oldest child not following Jesus, they found great help and support by sharing their burden with Christian friends. Knowing that others were praying for her and for her daughter was a great comfort.

But it is not always those who are of the family of faith that are the greatest support. Lisa says she experiences a sense of failure— "on an almost daily basis"—as a mother. This comes from the personality differences among her children and from the push and pull of raising them and launching them into adulthood. What helps her most, she says, is sharing her experiences with other women she respects. But she confesses that she often receives more support and encouragement from her non-Christian friends, who exhibit a level of honesty and "realness" that goes far beyond the platitudes she has too often experienced within the Christian community. That honesty and support has been a means of grace that God has used in Lisa's life.

In summary, it is through meditating on Scripture, individual and communal prayer, mutually honest and loving relationships, and many other spiritual disciplines that we can seek to connect our heads and our hearts, so that we might embrace and live out God's truth and grace as we respond to failure.

Keep On Pressing On

The writers of the New Testament often speak of a life of following God as a race (for example, 1 Cor 9:24-26; 2 Tim 4:7; Heb 12:1-2). Our lives are a race to be run to the end. Contrary to the standards of Vince Lombardi, the key thing that God is concerned about is not "winning" the race, but finishing it.[25]

When my daughter, Beth, ran the Chicago Marathon, her prime concern was not her time. She wanted to finish the race—and she did! I know a physician who is also a marathoner. One day one of his patients said to him, "I understand you ran the marathon yesterday." The doctor smiled and said yes. The patient continued, "That's twenty-six miles, isn't it?" My friend responded, "No, it's 26.2 miles. And don't forget that last 0.2. It's the hardest 0.2 miles you have ever run!"[26] The point is that to finish a marathon, you need to run all the way to the end. Similarly, you and I will not finish the race of life if we quit the course after a failure. Because the goal is to finish the race, we need to pick ourselves up off the ground and keep on running.

The Experience of David

In chapter four, we considered the experience of King David and his great failure stemming from his adultery with Bathsheba and his arranging the subsequent murder of her husband, Uriah.[27] It was a horrific collection of sins—the abuse of power at its very worst. David's initial response was like that of so many of us. He wanted to cover it up, to keep his guilt private and unknown behind a happy and successful façade.

David did cover up his sin at first. But God would not let him continue in this charade. God is not at all impressed with our exterior lives, no matter how bright they look, when they are different from what is going on in the heart. So in his relentless mercy, God sent the prophet Nathan to "speak truth to power" and confront the king.

Nathan told David a simple story about a rich man who stole from a poor man the only ewe lamb he owned. This story drew David in to the point that when Nathan specifically confronted the king ("You are the man!"), David understood his guilt. By the grace of God, he was empowered to come clean and confess his sin: "I have sinned against the LORD." Immediately, Nathan replied with God's forgiving mercy, but he also told David of the consequences of his sin that would remain: "The LORD has taken away your sin. You are not going to die. But because by doing this you have shown utter contempt for the LORD, the son born to you will die" (2 Sam 12:13-14).

When his son became sick, David pled with God for his child's life. He fasted for days, lying on the ground in sackcloth (a traditional sign of repentance and mourning). His anguish was so acute that when the child finally died, David's servants debated whether to even tell him. They were not at all sure how he might respond to such devastating news.

In fact, David's response was surprising. After hearing the news, "David got up from the ground. After he had washed, put on lotions and changed his clothes, he went into the house of the LORD and worshiped. Then he went to his own house, and at his request they served him food, and he ate" (2 Sam 12:20). He told his servants that while his child was still alive, he fasted and prayed fervently in the hope that God might choose to be gracious and heal him. But now that his child was dead, it was time to move on.

David's experience reveals two unhealthy ways of responding to failure in our lives. Some of us are like David before he was confronted by Nathan the prophet. We respond to our failures through denial, avoidance and hiding. We keep quiet, not wanting to tell the messy story of our failure, lest it shatter the image of ourselves we want to project to the world. We keep on nursing the wounds of our failure until we rationalize it away, or we end up convincing ourselves that it really wasn't our fault at all. Surely it was someone else's, we say. But whatever the specifics, we remain stuck—stuck in self-denial and hypocrisy.

Others of us struggle to get to the point David did after the death of his son—the ability to move forward. Those of us in this situation know our guilt all too well. We feel the pain and the disappointment deeply. We immerse ourselves so much in the narrative of our failure that we find ourselves unable to move on to the rest of the story—the good news of forgiveness and hope through the gospel. Having fallen down, we can't seem to pick ourselves up to continue the race.

While I don't in any way deny the need and the value of grieving our failures and our losses (Eccles 3:4 tells us there is a time to weep and mourn, even as there is a time to laugh and to dance), there does come a time when we need to get up off the ground and get back in the race. We need to follow the example of Paul and forget "what is behind" so that we can "press on toward the goal" that God has set for us (Phil 3:13-14).[28] Some of us reading this book (perhaps many of us) need to realize that it is time to get up, to wash ourselves and change our clothes, and to give ourselves again to the business of life—worshiping, loving and serving.

Queen Victoria was the longest reigning British monarch in history, reigning over the United Kingdom for sixty-three years and seven months (1837-1901). Her husband, Prince Albert, died in 1861. Upon his death, Queen Victoria entered a state of mourning. She wore black for the remainder of her life (forty years). She avoided public appearances and rarely set foot in London. Her seclusion earned her the nickname "The Widow of Windsor."[29] Though mourning and grief over the death of one's spouse is surely appropriate and important, forty years does seem like a bit much. Queen Victoria was stuck, unable to move on. May that not be the case with us.

When We Fail

So when we fail, what should we do? We need to confess any sin that might be involved in the failure, remembering that there might not be any sin at all. But if there is, it needs to be confessed. We need to consciously receive God's forgiveness and cleansing. We need to be assured of our continued standing as beloved children of God and to rest in his love. We need to grieve our mistakes appropriately but steadfastly refuse to wallow in them. And we need to get up and get back into the race.

As we do so, we need to acknowledge the reality of risk and of future failure as we continue to run. But we also need to realize that there is no failure like that of refusing to keep on running. Novelist and professor Walt Wangerin captured this perfectly. While he was originally speaking about risk and failure in ministry, his words apply to every area of life: "I am convinced that we are not called upon to succeed at anything in ministry. We are called upon to love. Which is to say, we are called upon to fail—both vigorously and joyfully."[30]

As we keep on loving and failing—vigorously and joyfully—we can sense the smile of God and know that it will be worth it in the end. It was for Jesus. And it will be for us as well.

Fix Our Eyes on Jesus

The author of Hebrews pointed to one additional factor that is necessary for us to be able to persevere in the race God sets for us. We must fix our eyes on Jesus.

> Therefore, since we are surrounded by such a great cloud of witnesses, let us throw off everything that hinders and the sin that so easily entangles. And let us run with perseverance the race marked out for us, *fixing our eyes on Jesus*, the pioneer and perfecter of faith. For the joy set before him he endured the cross, scorning the shame and sat down at the right hand of God. (Heb 12:1-2, emphasis added)

As we learn how to respond to failure, it is especially important for us to keep our eyes on Jesus, for he experienced the kind of rejection that would readily be identified as failure from a human perspective. Yet at the same time, his is ultimately the story of tremendous success. What a composite picture we get of

Jesus from Scripture—the success of a "failure"!

During the last week of his earthly life, Jesus told a story to describe all that would happen to him in the next few days. It's a story that speaks of rejection, suffering, death, vindication, resurrection. It's recorded in Matthew 21:33-46, Mark 12:1-13 and Luke 20:9-19.

There was a landowner who planted a vineyard and lovingly cared for it. He rented it out to tenant farmers, who were to tend the vines and make them as productive as possible. But when the time came for the owner to collect his crops, the tenants refused to give him what was rightly his. They repeatedly abused those sent to collect the crops. Finally the owner sent his son, thinking that the tenants would certainly respect him. On the contrary, the tenants killed the son, longing for the inheritance of the owner to belong to them. In response, the owner of the vineyard did two things: he brought judgment on the tenants, and he exalted and honored his son. Jesus made this very clear by quoting an evocative passage from the Old Testament as the climax to his story. He said, "The stone the builders rejected has become the cornerstone; / The Lord has done this, and it is marvelous in our eyes" (Mk 12:10-11).

This statement originally comes from Psalm 118:22-23. Psalm 118 is the conclusion of a group of six psalms sung by the Jews every year during their celebration of the Feast of Passover. In fact, it is very likely that this was one of the psalms Jesus and his disciples sang after celebrating the Last Supper on the night before he died (Mk 14:26). Psalm 118 celebrates the love and care that God has for his people. This was supremely demonstrated in the Exodus when God delivered his people from their slavery in Egypt. Though the Israelites had been rejected by the Egyptians, much as builders might reject a stone that they deem to be flawed, they were not rejected by their God. He worked powerfully to liberate them and to lead them to their own land. He vindicated and ex-

alted them, so much so that in the imagery of Psalm 118, they
became the cornerstone—the single most important stone in the
entire building.

When Jesus quoted these verses, he was not thinking of the nation of Israel as a whole. He knew himself to be the son who was
sent by his heavenly Father (the landowner) to the people of Israel
(the vineyard) and their religious leaders (the tenant farmers).[31]
But rather than being respected and honored as the son of the
landowner, Jesus would also be rejected. This had already been
the case.[32] And things would only get worse that coming week.

In this parable, Jesus predicted not only his rejection but also
his death. The tenants of the vineyard would kill the owner's son
and throw him out of the vineyard. And so it happened. Jesus'
crucifixion was a profound act of public disgrace and humiliation.
He was rejected by the Jewish religious leaders, by Roman officials
and even by his closest followers. Jesus was betrayed by Judas, and
three times Peter denied even knowing him. The rest of his followers all fled in fear for their lives. Following his "conviction" by a
cowardly Roman ruler, Jesus endured mocking, beating, flogging
and ultimately the agonizing death of crucifixion. And in his final
conscious moments, he felt abandoned and forsaken by the one
who all his life was the closest to him, his Father in heaven, and
he cried out, "My God, my God, why have you forsaken me?" (Mt
27:46; Mk 15:34).[33]

Truly, Jesus was the stone the builders rejected. Three long,
hard years of ministry had culminated in Jesus being rejected by
the leaders of his people and abandoned by his friends. Ultimately,
as he hung on the cross, he was stripped of all his dignity, even as
he was stripped of all his clothing. No management consultant
would ever have looked at Jesus on the cross that Friday and
deemed him a success. How can you be a success when everyone
rejects you?[34]

But this is only the human perspective.[35] In reality, not everyone rejected him. The ultimate significant other, God himself, saw everything Jesus did. He knew that his Son was and had always been faithful to him. He knew that the rejection of others was in no way the result of sin on his part. The Father looked deep into Jesus' heart and was delighted in his Son. And he did something about it. He raised Jesus from the dead in vindication and triumph.

> The stone the builders rejected has become the cornerstone;
> The Lord has done this, and it is marvelous in our eyes.

This is the heart of the good news! God looked at his beloved son, who had experienced failure from a human perspective, and deemed him a success. God saw the faithfulness of his Son and vindicated him by raising him from the dead.[36] It is, and should be seen as, *marvelous* in our eyes.

It is marvelous that Jesus Christ experienced rejection and shame. That makes him able to empathize with us when we go through similar experiences. When we are rejected, when we fail to accomplish our hopes and dreams, Jesus knows how it feels.[37] The New Testament letter to the Hebrews describes him in terms of the Jewish high priest—the one who was charged to help the people in their relationship to God. The author said that Jesus is our high priest, one who can sympathize with us in all we go through, precisely because he has experienced all the various temptations we face (including those that come from our experiences of rejection and failure). And because he has been tempted, he is able to help us whenever we need it (Heb 4:15-16).

This principle and its connection to the promise of Psalm 118 is also made by the apostle Peter. Peter and John healed a crippled beggar who had been lame from birth (Acts 3:1-10). This caused quite a stir within the city of Jerusalem, and the Jewish elders and teachers of the law had Peter and John brought before them. "By what power or in what name did you do this?" they asked. Peter responded,

> Rulers and elders of the people! If we are being called to account today for an act of kindness shown to a man who was lame and are being asked how he was healed, then know this, you and all the people of Israel: It is by the name of Jesus Christ of Nazareth, whom you crucified but whom God raised from the dead, that this man stands before you healed. Jesus is
>
> > "the stone you builders rejected,
> > which has become the cornerstone." (Acts 4:8-11)

Because God raised Jesus from the dead, this rejected stone has become the cornerstone. This is why Jesus Christ had the power to heal crippled beggars in the book of Acts. And because Jesus has been raised from the dead, he has the power today to heal us from brokenness and shame and pain. He has the power to redeem our failures. He has the power to make us, even as he was, genuinely successful in the eyes of God.

So as we confront failure, rejection, hurt and shame, which all of us experience, we need to fix our eyes on Jesus. He is our model.[38] He is our healer. He is the one who forgives us and cleanses us. He is the one who will love us forever with his everlasting love. And he alone can empower us to run with perseverance the race marked out for us.

8

Helping Others

ℭℛ

As we move toward the close of this book, I want to reflect briefly on some of the ways we can help others cope with failure in their lives.

If it is true that all of us will experience failure and that it's not a question of *if*, but of *when* and *how*, then by extension this is true not only for ourselves but also for all those people God brings into our lives. And we want to help them cope. This is a natural, God-given instinct. It's normal and right—part of loving our neighbors as we love ourselves.

As I write these reflections, I am especially mindful of those God has called to help his people as pastors and church leaders. This is not surprising, given my former twelve-year ministry as a pastor and my current vocation of teaching and equipping future pastors. The bulk of what I will say in this chapter is especially addressed to my fellow pastors. I also believe that what I have to say will be helpful in one way or another for all Christians, since all of us are called by God to love others and to seek to help them in whatever ways we can.

So, how can we help others in their experience of failure? How can we pastors be faithful shepherds in these times of great need? The reflections that follow are by no means meant to be comprehensive in scope. They are intentionally brief and suggestive rather than fully discussed. And they are presented in no particular order. Many of these ideas have been explored at various points in this book already. But it will be helpful to draw together these various strands so we might gain needed guidance in the task of loving and helping others as they grapple with failure.

Your Example Matters

Every person who is called to be a leader of God's people, whether she or he occupies a formal, public position of leadership within a congregation or exercises informal and individual leadership with friends, neighbors and coworkers, is called on to be an example (1 Tim 4:12; 1 Pet 5:3; 1 Cor 11:1). This is true in all of life, but in few areas is it more important than in dealing with failure. We must model wise and healthy ways of coping with failure. The value of the ministry of modeling cannot be overstated.

One area in which this pastoral example is perhaps most crucial involves our honesty and transparency about our own failures. I have already noted that admitting our failures openly and grappling with them honestly is important for all of us as we seek to respond to failure in a healthy way. Nothing is more effective in helping people to be open and honest about their failures than seeing a similar kind of openness and honesty on the part of their leaders. Authenticity and vulnerability on our part make it easier to follow our example. These are virtues more readily caught than taught.

If those seeking to lead and help others retreat into silence and are unwilling or unable to share their failures, their struggles, their sin, their questions and their doubts, it is highly unlikely that those they seek to influence will grow in these areas. Perhaps a leader feels that he or she needs to keep up a certain kind of image—that of being godly, growing and successful. This desire might be motivated by pride and a longing to be acclaimed for what the image portrays. Other times it may arise out of a fear that our real self will be viewed by others as unacceptable and unworthy.[1] But sometimes the desire can feel nobler. A leader can be tempted to feel that if she or he would only keep up this image, those who follow would be helped more. But this is a myth—a dangerous myth.

In his very helpful book for Christian leaders, *Leadership as an Identity*, Crawford Loritts wrote, "It's a dangerous thing to follow a leader who has never failed. Let's be honest: Anyone who claims to have never failed has a character problem—lying."[2] But not only does an unwillingness to admit to failure constitute a problematic lack of honesty on our part, it also robs those in the congregation of a critical example to follow. If we as leaders are unwilling to be open about our failures and the various ways (both helpful and not so helpful) that we have tried to cope with them, we fail to lead others by authentic and genuine example.

After Susan and I returned from a leave of absence we had taken to help us process the crisis we had been experiencing in our ministry in the Pacific Northwest (see chapter one), we spoke together to our congregation during a Sunday evening service. We sought to be very open and honest about the nature of our issues, the various factors that led to them, what we had been learning and the process of growth we had begun. This kind of pastoral openness was a new thing for our congregation (our church secretary commented that she had never heard such openness from a pastor during her lifetime in church). I consider this fact with some degree of shame. I had been the pastor of the church for more than three and a half years. No doubt there had been other opportunities for such openness and transparency. But I was in process (as we all are), and it was only then, in the midst of a time of crisis, that I was ready and willing to be that honest. Many in the congregation commented on how helpful that was.

To be sure, congregational leaders need wisdom as to whom to share with, how much to disclose and when.[3] Those who are called to preach should not use the pulpit as an ongoing confessional or personal therapy session. Their preaching and teaching, after all, is not ultimately about them, but rather about God and his grace. Pastoral counselor Jerry Law says that pastors in the pulpit are to be translucent (letting the light of Christ shine) while being appropriately transparent (revealing their life situations).[4] Transparency regarding our experiences of failure can involve issues that rightly need to be kept confidential, and congregational leaders need to respect the effects of their disclosure on others. But so many leaders go to the opposite extreme and rarely, if ever, admit their failures, their struggles, their sins, their questions. If they do, they admit them only after there has been a somewhat positive resolution to the situation. And the congregations they shepherd are the poorer for it.

Your Preaching Matters

When life is shaken to its core due to failures, we need a sure and solid foundation to stand on. For us as Christians, this foundation consists of central truths of Scripture that we have been talking about in this book—truths about the nature of failure, the universality of failure, our human finiteness and the inevitability of risk, the grace of God that we can experience in the midst of failure, and God's ultimate and eternal triumph. We all need to learn, internalize and rest in these great truths of grace. One of the greatest privileges and responsibilities of pastors and other church leaders is to help lay that foundation accurately and strongly.

This privilege does not belong to pastors alone. The apostle

Paul wrote in his letter to the Colossians, "Let the message of Christ dwell among you richly as you teach and admonish one another with all wisdom" (Col 3:16). This is a great opportunity for all of us to help each other. All of us are able to pass on the truths of God's Word that have shaped us. All of us can share our experience of how these truths of grace have supported and helped us in a time of need. All of us can encourage and exhort one another.[5] Paul calls us to do this "with all wisdom," and Scripture stresses that God is eager to give such wisdom to his children when they ask him for it (Jas 1:5).

However, the work of foundation-laying is especially significant for those God has called to preach and teach his word regularly. Pastors have been granted the unspeakable privilege of proclaiming and teaching the inspired, God-breathed Scriptures. And Paul is very clear about the value of the Word of God: "All Scripture is God-breathed and is useful for teaching, rebuking, correcting and training in righteousness, so that all God's people may be thoroughly equipped for every good work" (2 Tim 3:16-17). Certainly included in these "good works" are ways in which we cope wisely and well with failure.

The time to help lay this foundation is now—before failure comes and its traumatic impact is felt so deeply. Those of us who are called by God to preach and teach his Word need to include these themes regularly and consistently. We must avoid the triumphalist versions of Christian faith that are all too common for North American Christians in the twenty-first century. These approaches to the faith trumpet success as if it were the expected norm to which we are entitled as children of God, while they keep strangely silent about the realities of failure, suffering, sin and doubt.

But this is not the message of Scripture. We need to be honest about failure—honest in speaking from our own lives, honest about the reality of struggle, pain and failure in the lives of our congregation, and honest with respect to the Scriptures. We need to assure our congregants that our failures do not take God by surprise. They do not disqualify us from his love and care. They will not have the last word in our lives, for God is in the business of redeeming our failures and using them to transform us. What a privilege it is to help lay that foundation right now. For if we can help to lay a firm and secure foundation in advance, the people we serve will be much better equipped to cope with failure wisely and well.

Your Praying Matters

In the previous chapter, we talked about the crucial role of prayer in seeking to live out biblical truth and grace with regard to our failures. This transformative spiritual practice is a crucial part of coping wisely and well with failure. This is true not only for the prayers we pray for ourselves; it is also true for prayers we pray on behalf of others. This kind of intercessory prayer is one of the greatest ways we can love one another. Certainly this is a role that pastors and spiritual shepherds ought to regularly engage in on behalf of those they serve. We need to be praying regularly for the members of the flock privately and together with them in a whole host of contexts.

Many times I can be tempted to think that the most important words I can bring into a situation of failure involving someone I love are the words I speak to them. These words are crucial, but how often does my elevation of their importance betray my prideful opinion of my ability to know and speak the right words that can "fix" a situation. And how often does my preoccupation with the words I speak evidence a practical lack of faith in the power of God and in the value of prayer. In the final analysis, the words I speak to God on behalf of the members of my flock are ultimately far more important and far more valuable than any words I might speak to them.

It is also valuable to consider how spiritual shepherds can incorporate prayer into the corporate worship of God's people. Pastor and professor Craig Barnes has written eloquently about the privilege he has of leading the congregation in prayer during corporate worship, calling it "the most important thing I do" for them.[6] As he leads in prayer, he places the church back in God's hands. And, he asks, what could be more powerful than that?

Barnes says that his goal as he leads in prayer is to keep the conversation going between his people and their God. One of the crucial functions of such praying is to help people name the issues in their lives and to give them language and categories to be able to speak to God about them. This is a crucial help for all of us as we struggle to tell the truth to God about our struggles and pain, our failures and losses, our guilt and our grief and our doubts. Prayer provides a safe place to surrender to God the marriage that is faltering, the financial pressure that seems overwhelming, the failures felt so deeply on the job or with children. Barnes says that when the prayer is done, he longs for his people to be thinking, "Yes, that is what I wanted to tell God, but I didn't know how to say it."[7]

In addition, pastors and worship planners can provide space in corporate worship for the members of their congregations to offer themselves and their concerns to God. Our pastor of worship and the arts at LaSalle Street Church, Gary Rand, excels at this. We pray regularly in our corporate worship, in a whole host of ways—corporately, being led by our pastors in prayer, often in response to individual sharing of needs and concerns, and through a variety of forms of silent prayer in the corporate worship context. Throughout the Lenten season last year, we had several opportunities to write prayer requests on pieces of fabric and lay them on the cross. And during our Easter celebration, we had the chance to pray for the experience of resurrection in our lives and families by attaching a flower to the cross. Such creative opportunities create space and provide ways for us to bring even our hardest issues to the God of all grace as we gather to worship him.

Your Presence Matters

One of the consequences we often experience as a result of our failures is shame. In our shame, we come to feel that our failures have made us unacceptable as persons—unacceptable to God and unacceptable to others. But when we as pastors and spiritual helpers are able to be present with those we love in their failures, we communicate very powerfully not only our love and acceptance, but also God's. On these occasions, it is "the ministry of presence" that is so powerful and so healing. Far more than any words we might say, our "being there" can communicate love tangibly and powerfully. Even if our teaching and preaching is biblically accurate and wise, even if we are honest and transparent about our own struggles and efforts to cope, if it is all done long-distance, the impact is greatly minimized. Those grappling with failure, and especially with the shame that can accompany it, need the presence of those who love them.[8]

The Gospel of Mark records an incident in the early days of Jesus' ministry when he healed a man with leprosy. In the Bible, the word translated *leprosy* refers to a whole group of infectious skin diseases, with varying degrees of severity. At its worst, leprosy was disfiguring, contagious, incurable and fatal. In the ancient world, there was only one known way to cope with this dreaded disease: quarantine. In Leviticus 13:45-46, we read the Old Testament regulations requiring lepers to live alone outside the city. To prevent any accidental contamination, the leper had to cry out "Unclean! Unclean!" whenever anyone approached. It doesn't take much imagination to realize that the psychological and emotional effects of this enforced isolation were every bit as devastating as the physical effects of leprosy, and perhaps more so.

When this man came to Jesus, he fell to his knees and begged him, "If you are willing, you can make me clean" (Mk 1:40). The text goes on to record that Jesus was indignant (perhaps angry at the physical and emotional toll of such a disease or perhaps angry because of the doubt expressed by this man about Jesus' willingness to heal).[9] But "[Jesus] reached out his hand and touched the man. 'I am willing,' he said. 'Be clean!' Immediately the leprosy left him and he was cleansed" (Mk 1:41-42).

This is a wonderful miracle, a marvelous testimony to the mighty healing power of Jesus. But I am drawn to the fact that before Jesus healed this man, he reached out his hand and touched him. This action was against the Jewish ceremonial laws; healthy Jews were supposed to stay far away from lepers. Even an accidental touch of a person with leprosy would render one ceremonially unclean. Yet Jesus drew near and intentionally touched this man *before* he healed him.[10] I'm convinced that this simple action communicated more love and care and acceptance by Jesus than any of his words ever could. His touch was every bit as crucial in the overall healing and restoration of this man as the physical healing itself.

In the previous chapter, we considered the recurring metaphor in Scripture of a race to describe our lives as followers of Jesus. Writer Anne Lamott vividly described her experience of watching Special Olympics track and field events. Not infrequently, the Special Olympians would stop running in the middle of a race, for a variety of reasons. Sometimes they would just sit down on the track and even start to take off their shoes or clothes. But these runners would not stay in the dust.

Every single one of them has been assigned a volunteer, and that person steps out from the sidelines and goes to the runner, and gets down on the ground with him or her and helps him or her put the shoes and clothes back on, and then takes the person by the hand and they start off again toward the finish line. In all the years I've been going, I've never once seen someone not get over the finish line.[11]

These volunteers help Special Olympians get back on their feet and finish the race in a host of ways. But perhaps none is more meaningful as getting down on the ground with them. Watching the Special Olympics reminded Lamott of all the "volunteers" God had provided for her as a single mom when she regularly found herself "down in the dirt." This is what God calls us to be for each other when failure drives us to the ground.

This is especially true for pastors and church leaders. We need to be present with those who have been laid off from their jobs. Our presence can communicate that we still value and love them, and that they still have much to contribute to the lives of others within the church and in the broader community, even as they are grieving, processing and searching for another job.

We need to be present with those who have gone through the trauma of divorce. No matter what the specifics of the issues involved, these people need to know of our love for them. The dignity, value and worth of our divorced friends need to be affirmed and expressed. And nothing communicates this more powerfully than our presence.

We need to be present with those who have experienced moral failure. Our ministry of presence does not condone their sin. It is not incompatible with our role of calling people to appropriate repentance, confession, restitution and reconciliation. But it is a way we can seek to live out the familiar maxim "Hate the sin and love the sinner." Evangelical pastors tend to do a better job of hating the sin than we do of loving the sinner. Often this comes from our efforts to engage in pastoral ministry long-distance. From the pulpit, we can readily denounce sin. We can make lofty moral pronouncements about issues that seemingly are clear-cut. No one will doubt our commitment to holiness and high moral standards from the way we preach. But genuinely loving the person caught in sin demands the closeness of relationship. It is much more complex and messy. At times, our efforts to genuinely love and support and encourage those caught in sin can be interpreted as being too lenient, accommodating and morally lax.

This has been the charge recently leveled against Christians involved with the Fellowship, a Washington, D.C., ministry that seeks to support and encourage the faith of politicians and other powerful people in our nation's capital.[12] In a D.C. row house that the group has used for Bible study and prayer groups, the "C Street House," members of the Fellowship have sought to support Senator John Ensign of Nevada and Governor Mark Sanford of South Carolina after their well-publicized extramarital affairs. The support did not come at the expense of calls to moral obedience; indeed one resident of the C Street House learned of both affairs and tried to talk each politician into ending them. But residents of this house and others in the Fellowship have sought to be present and to minister to these politicians who have failed morally by their encouragement, prayer and emotional support. This grace that has been given has scandalized others. Reverend Rob Schenk of Faith and Action, another Washington, D.C., ministry, wonders if the residents of the C Street House might have been too accommodating about the foibles and sins of its residents and friends, so as to attract the famous and powerful to its ministries. "We're [all] tempted to make room for their weaknesses," he commented.[13]

Clearly this is a complex situation, and I am in no position to evaluate the motives and actions of those involved. Without question, sin needs to be confronted, and those engaged in such practices need to be called to repentance. Clearly the wives of these politicians and other family members who have been hurt so deeply need to be supported and cared for. But loving grace for those who have sinned, the kind that can seem scandalous, needs to be there in abundance as well. There can be no doubt that this is what Jesus calls us to do—to love our neighbor, even our sinning neighbor, as ourselves. This demands our presence.

As we seek to love genuinely those grappling with failure, we must remember that our choice of words matters. While they can never be a substitute for our ministry of presence, our words of love and affirmation do have value. Our dilemma as Christian leaders is that we have so often been conditioned to be the people with the answers. We feel the need to say the right thing to bring about growth and healing. But just giving answers is not genuine love.

Foundational truths from Scripture are helpful for all of us as we grapple with failure. But the preferred time to work through these is in advance of the failure or sufficiently past the immediate crisis so as to provide space for learning, exploration and discovery. In the immediacy of the moment, what is needed most is our presence and our words of affirmation and love: "I am so sorry this has happened. I can only begin to imagine how much it hurts. But I want you to know that I love you, and far more important, God loves you. And I will be here with you as you work through this."

One final thought about these vital, life-giving relationships. Pastors and church leaders need to help foster them in abundance. No matter how important a pastor's ministry of presence is, no matter how critical his or her prayers and words of affirmation and encouragement might be, they are not enough. No pastor has time to be present with all who are struggling to cope with their failure. No matter how much time he or she can invest in relationships, others will be needed as well.

This means that every pastor needs to be intentional and strategic about fostering possibilities for interdependent relationships among the members of their congregations. Whether these relationships come through small groups or other committed accountability structures, or are fostered more casually and informally, there is no substitute for Christians loving one another, bearing one another's burdens, encouraging and exhorting one another, and praying for each other.[14] These relationships of mutual love and care are absolutely crucial as we travel together on the journey of faith through the deep valleys of our failures.

Your Focus Matters

As critical as your preaching and prayers and presence are, as critical as mutually loving and caring relationships undoubtedly are, none of these is the most important element in helping us cope with failure in our lives. Jesus is.

Above all else, we need to fix our eyes on Jesus. He is our model for dealing with failure. He is our healer, the one who alone can take away our shame and forgive our sins. He is the one who will redeem our failures and transform our lives. He is our reconciler—with God and with others. He is the one who will love us with an everlasting love. He is the one who can motivate us and move us and empower us to pick ourselves up off the ground and to keep pressing on. There is no one else.

So perhaps the most important word I have for those who are called to lead and to shepherd God's people is a very simple one. Yet it is very profound. Keep Jesus central. Keep him as the focus of your life and your ministry. He is the Son of God who comes to us from the Father "full of grace and truth" (Jn 1:14). As we keep

Jesus central, we also keep ourselves centered in his grace and in his truth. And there is nothing that can ultimately help and strengthen us and our people as we grapple with failure more than the grace and truth of Jesus.[15]

As pastors, it is all too easy to find another center to our ministry. Rather than being radically Christ-centered, we can become program-centered, whether the ministry programs are well-planned and well-executed worship services, vibrant youth groups, shelters and soup kitchens, or child-care centers. We often end up reducing the God of all grace and truth to a program that we seek to carry out in our own strength and for our own glory.

Or we can become cause-centered in our ministry—focusing on social justice or prolife issues or education funding or creation care or racial reconciliation. No doubt, these issues are crucial ones and faithfulness to Jesus Christ demands thoughtful and challenging involvement with them all. But if in the end we are more oriented to the issues of justice than to the God of justice, we get the cart before the horse and we lose sight of the only one who can motivate and energize our engagement in the long run, the only one who can forgive us for our failures.[16]

Sometimes we can become more theology-centered than Christ-centered or gospel-centered. As a theology professor, I can be tempted with this. At the end of the day, am I more concerned with my theology of God or with the God of my theology? We need to ask ourselves whether our specific doctrinal convictions are ultimately more central to our lives and ministries than the Christ-centered core message of the New Testament.

No doubt there are positive benefits to all these emphases. They can and they should be a part of our ministries. But all too often they end up squeezing out Jesus as the ultimate center and focus of our efforts to help others. If we allow the good to become the enemy of the best, our people will be impoverished.

For, in the end, it is only as we and those around us fix our eyes on Jesus that all of us can join together and keep on running the race marked out for us. Only with our eyes fixed on Jesus can we grow through our failures more and more to reflect our Maker and Redeemer.

Epilogue

I began this book by recounting a significant and painful crisis of success and failure that Susan and I experienced in our pastoral ministry in the Pacific Northwest. In many ways, this book is a reflection on a lifelong process of struggle and growth in dealing with our questions. So it seems appropriate to return to my own journey and to share more of what has been helpful to me.

While Susan and I learned much as a result of our crisis in 1992 and its aftermath, my struggles in these areas have not ended. My experience has reflected the reality that transformation is never completed this side of heaven. There have been challenging seasons throughout my journey, in which I have been confronted with failure and ways of coping with it wisely and well. Some have been professional—the decision to leave pastoral ministry in the church in the Pacific Northwest (two and a half years after the crisis we described), the transition to doctoral studies that followed and the job search following the completion of my Ph.D. God was gracious and ultimately led us to my current teaching position, but not without many anxious moments about the realities of finding a job and the impact this might have on our family.

There have been relational challenges as Susan and I moved from the complementary ministries of pastor and pastor's wife to the separate vocations and roles we now have. We have transitioned through some life stages in our family and sought to navigate the impact they have had on our relationships and roles as parents and spouses. Even the process of writing this book has raised many issues.

Through all these situations, the prospect of failure was very real. Success seemed to fluctuate between a tantalizingly close reality and a distant ideal. I have studied and meditated on the truths of grace that I shared in chapters five and six, and they have brought me comfort and hope on many occasions. But they have also been a source of frustration, as I have grieved my inability to internalize them and live them out. Far too often my life has reflected Paul's agony in Romans 7 (for example, Rom 7:19, "I do not do the good I want to do, but the evil I do not want to do—this I keep on doing").

But God has been faithful. Not by eliminating failure—not yet. But he has drawn near and supported me throughout my journey. He has allowed me to struggle, and he has helped me in the struggle to cope with my failures in ways he would desire. God has met me again and again in his Word and in prayer. He has given me the great privilege of being able to teach the truths of grace in his Word again and again. I pray that those I've taught from pulpits and in Sunday school and seminary classrooms have benefited even half as much as I have. Certainly their responses and their questions have refined my thinking again and again. But perhaps most of all, God has met me and strengthened me and encouraged me through the people he has brought into my life.

I have already shared the seminal experience of meeting with and being helped by Jack Harrison. That experience caused Susan and me to appreciate the incredibly valuable role counselors can play, so

much so that in a later season of stress involving doctoral studies
and a job search, we sought out another counselor. He too was a very
significant helper, mentor and channel of God's grace to us.

During another season of grappling with failure, I began to
meet regularly for breakfast once a week with a member of our
Sunday school class. His presence in my life communicated the
acceptance I needed. And the prayers and accountability we shared
were invaluable.

Faculty and staff colleagues at the seminary where I teach
have also been a tremendous support. Our seminary dean has
modeled humble, persevering faithfulness in the midst of the
challenges of his vocation and he has shown an open hospitality
that has greatly encouraged me. Members of my department
have given me a rare combination of pastoral care and friendship, encouragement in my life and vocation, and challenges to
keep growing and learning.

Susan and I are privileged to be members of LaSalle Street
Church in Chicago. This amazing congregation has modeled for
us what it means to be open about our brokenness and to accept
one another in Christ, no matter where we are. We love the honesty of this fellowship, the diversity of its members and their issues, and its willingness to embrace the joys and challenges and
all the messiness of life in relationship with God and each other.

Our pastor, Laura Truax, has been a model of transparent vulnerability and of extending grace to all she meets. We are the
grateful beneficiaries of her vision and her preaching. She finds
ways again and again in our diverse urban congregation to be
present and to provide faithful pastoral care. She and the entire
LaSalle community have been invaluable partners to us as we have
learned about failure.

And finally, I would be remiss if I did not mention my family
and the role they have played in my life. My parents have mod-

eled God's love in wonderful ways in their relationship with one another and with our whole family. This past summer our extended family gathered to rejoice in their love and faithfulness to one another as Mom and Dad celebrated their sixtieth wedding anniversary. I saw this love in action this spring as my mom has been recovering from surgery. The care my father has shown to her has demonstrated again and again the kind of faithful love that characterizes our heavenly Father. To the extent that I am able to internalize God's love for me, it is owing mostly to the love of my dad.

Our three children—Andrew, Beth and Lydia—and their spouses have also shown me faithful love. We have laughed together, cried together and grown up together. It has been a joy to watch and participate in each of their weddings. And now Susan and I have the privilege and challenge of parenting adult children and relating to them in ways that befit their new status and ours.

Finally, without question, Susan has been the single most significant person God has used in my life to help me learn to cope with failure. In the closeness of our marriage, we have struggled with our differences as people and with the different dimensions of our individual journeys. But throughout, we have sought to "do different together." I have talked more about issues of success and failure with Susan than with anyone else. And I've experienced both of these realities with her. No one knows my failures as she does (and vice versa), and no one rejoices in my successes as she does. She has helped me see that my failures are not an end. She encourages me not to cave in to them. And she reminds me that I can get up and start over again. She has helped me see the goodness of the unique person God created me to be.

Together Susan and I have seen glimmers of the final hope that is ours as children of God. In relationship with Susan, as nowhere else, I regularly come to grips with the fact that I have not arrived by any means. But she is the one, above all others, that God has used to help me forget "what is behind and strain toward what is ahead" so that I can keep pressing on "toward the goal to win the prize for which God has called me heavenward in Christ Jesus" (Phil 3:13-14).

All of these people—and more—are means of grace God has, and is, using in my life to help me learn how to cope more effectively with my failures. And this is the opportunity we all have to help one another. We really do need one another. May God help us all to be this kind of friend and helper to each other.

Notes

Chapter 1: A Violinist and a Pastor

[1]The New Testament is very clear that Jesus Christ is the ultimate judge of all humanity. According to John 5:22-23, God the Father "has entrusted all judgment to the Son, that all may honor the Son as they honor the Father." And in Jesus' famous parable of the sheep and the goats in Matthew 25:31-46, all the nations of the world will appear before the Son of Man in his glory, and he is the one who will separate them as a shepherd separates the sheep from the goats. Christians as well will appear before Christ as the ultimate judge to be evaluated by him. Paul told the church in Corinth, "We must all appear before the judgment seat of Christ, that everyone may receive what is due them for the things done while in the body, whether good or bad" (2 Cor 5:10).

[2]The names and identifying details of people and situations in this and subsequent stories have been changed. The only exceptions to this practice are illustrations that come from news stories that have been reported by the media and those that come from published works.

[3]The modern church-growth movement can be traced to the insights of a missionary to India, Donald McGavran. His observations of various church-planting ministries in India caused him to investigate why some churches grow and multiply, while others stagnate and decline. After twenty-six years of studying these questions all over the world, in 1961 McGavran established the Institute of Church Growth at Northwest Christian College in Eugene, Oregon. Later that year, an annual Church Growth Seminar was established in Winona Lake, Indiana. In 1965, McGavran was named dean of the newly formed Graduate School of World Mission at Fuller Theological Seminary. In 1971, he published the definitive work on church growth, *Understanding Church Growth.*

(The third edition of this work was published by Eerdmans in 1990.) A colleague of McGavran's, C. Peter Wagner, helped to pioneer the use of the principles of church growth with reference to the church in America. For a helpful and succinct overview of the church-growth movement, see Donald A. McGavran, "Church Growth Movement," in *Evangelical Dictionary of Theology*, ed. Walter A. Elwell (Grand Rapids: Baker, 1984), pp. 241-43.

[4]Marva Dawn captured this sentiment as she looked at the way North American cultural understandings of success have impacted the practice of Christian worship in the United States and Canada in the 1990s. "As relationships, entertainment, and even the news become increasingly superficial, society looks for ways to signify success. Lacking any tools to grade quality, we have to measure quantity." This, she argued, has led to the pervasive and devastating influence of "the god of competition and the idolatry of numbers and success." Her comments are even more applicable a decade and a half later. *Reaching Out Without Dumbing Down: A Theology of Worship for the Turn-of-the-Century Culture* (Grand Rapids: Eerdmans, 1995), p. 51.

[5]Recently, some emergent and missional churches have reacted against this, stressing the intimacy of community life that smaller congregations can offer and the missional advantages that kind of community can bring. It is too soon to tell if this will be an enduring and long-term shift of perspective among American evangelicals.

[6]In Marshall Shelley, *Well-Intentioned Dragons: Ministering to Problem People in the Church* (Carol Stream, Ill.: Leadership/Word Books, 1985), p. 35.

Chapter 2: In Whose Eyes?

[1]Anthony Campolo Jr., *The Success Fantasy* (Wheaton, Ill.: Victor, 1980), p. 9. Campolo's statement about failure as our society's "unforgivable sin" is impressionistic and descriptive (and I think accurate). It is not intended to deal theologically with the relationship between failure and sin. That relationship will be explored more fully in chapters four and five.

[2]Merriam-Webster, "Success" <www.merriam-webster.com/dictionary/success>.

[3]Doug Firebaugh, "Success to Success—What is the Meaning of Success in Life?" <http://ezinearticles.com/?Success-to-Success---What-is-the-Meaning-of-Success-in-Life?&id=139160>.

[4]Campolo, *Success Fantasy*, p. 20.

[5]In contemporary usage, the term "significant other" often refers to a partner in a romantic, unmarried (often live-in) relationship. Yet it can profitably be used as I am using it in this chapter—to refer to a person or group toward whom we orient our behavior and whose opinion of us matters greatly in the way we view our own success or failure.

[6]Often our perception of what "everyone" is doing is not very accurate. This is a foundational conviction behind an approach to encouraging responsible behavior in the areas of smoking, drinking and drug use among high school and college students called "social norming." This approach is based on the conviction that young people's perceptions of what their peers are doing drives their behavior. This becomes especially problematic due to the fact that surveys show that they consistently overestimate the prevalence of high-risk behaviors among their peers. So they think "everyone" is engaged in a particular behavior. But this perception very often does not approach reality. For example, a 2006 survey in the high school where my wife used to work revealed that students thought that only 21 percent of their peers were alcohol-free during the last thirty days. Yet in the same survey, 71 percent of the students reported being alcohol-free in the last thirty days ("Teen Norms Survey Results Are Promising," Parent Article, Vernon Hills High School, Vernon Hills, Ill., December 2006). School administrators publicize these statistics widely (for example, through ubiquitous posters at school), hoping to change the perceptions of these young people and thus their behaviors. The crucial point for our purposes is that perceptions of the behaviors of peer groups that serve as significant others are not always accurate.

[7]Deborah Tannen chronicles the shift in power that comes when daughters reach adulthood. She says that "as a daughter's focus shifts (away from primary reliance on her mother), it may be the mother who deeply wants her daughter's approval—especially in our society, which places more value on the freshness of youth than on the wisdom of age. . . . And only her daughter can give her the ultimate stamp of approval: reassurance that she did a good job as a mother. In these ways, a mother is at her grown daughter's mercy, just as her children were at hers when they were small. The situation is compounded when a daughter has children of her own. Now it is the daughter who controls access to the grandchildren." *You're Wearing That? Understanding Mothers and Daughters in Conversation* (New York: Random House, 2006), p. 59.

[8]Pastor Laura S. Truax, "God's Offer and the Widow's Choice," sermon given at LaSalle Street Church, Chicago, November 9, 2008.

[9]Isaac Phiri and Joe Maxwell, "Gospel Riches: Africa's Rapid Embrace of Prosperity Pentecostalism Provokes Concern—and Hope," *Christianity Today*, July 2007, pp. 22-29. As one example, the authors cite Pastor Michael Okonkwo, bishop of the Redeemed Evangelical Mission since 1988: "Many are ignorant of the fact that God has already made provision for his children to be wealthy here on earth. When I say wealthy, I mean very, very rich. . . . Break loose! It's not a sin to desire to be wealthy" (p. 23).

[10]Lombardi's focus can be seen in some of his other quotes. For example, he said,

"If winning isn't everything, why do they keep score?" and "Show me a good loser, and I'll show you a loser" and "There is no room for second place. There is only one place in my game, and that is first place" (Brainy Quotes, "Vince Lombardi" <www.brainyquote.com/quotes/authors/v/vince_lombardi.html> [accessed November 5, 2008]).

[11]Reflecting on the numerous interviews she has had with mothers and daughters, Tannen said, "Nearly every mother I talked to said at some point that she worried about ways she had not been a good mother" (*You're Wearing That?* p. 138).

[12]On God as the Creator of all things, see Genesis 1:1; Exodus 20:11; Nehemiah 9:6; Acts 4:24; Colossians 1:16; Revelation 10:6. On God as the Creator of human beings, see Genesis 1:26-27; 2:7; Job 33:4; Psalm 139:13-16; Acts 17:24-26. On God as owner, see Psalms 24:1; 89:11; Colossians 1:16. On God as judge, see Matthew 25:31-32; Acts 17:30-31; 2 Corinthians 5:10; Revelation 20:11-12.

[13]Revelation 20:11-12 also speaks of the universality of God's judgment: "Then I saw a great white throne and him who was seated on it. The earth and the heavens fled from his presence, and there was no place for them. And I saw the dead, *great and small*, standing before the throne, and books were opened. Another book was opened, which is the book of life. The dead were judged according to what they had done as recorded in the books" (emphasis added).

[14]This is how Jesus lived during his life on earth. He said, "The one who sent me is with me; he has not left me alone, for I always do what pleases him" (Jn 8:29). That's why the author of Hebrews prays that the God of peace would work through Christ to produce in us "what is pleasing to him" (Heb 13:21).

[15]In my reflections on this text, I have been greatly helped by the discussion by John White in his *Daring to Draw Near* (Downers Grove, Ill.: InterVarsity Press, 1977), pp. 23-36.

[16]This same expression forms the climax of another parable of Jesus'. It is a parable about a wedding feast in which an invited guest presumes to sit in the place of honor. But when another more distinguished guest arrived, the person who exalted himself was asked to take the least important seat. How different is the situation of the humble guest who instinctively looks for the seat of lesser importance, only to have the host exalt her in the presence of all by inviting her to sit at a place of great honor. The lesson, according to Jesus, is that "all those who exalt themselves will be humbled, and those who humble themselves will be exalted" (Lk 14:11).

[17]Jesus' teaching on being a servant comes in response to the request from James and John to be seated in the two places closest to him in the coming fullness of the kingdom. Clearly they were seeking maximum glory and prestige for themselves. They wanted the status and limelight that would inevitably come from

being the "closest" to Jesus. And the other disciples were no different. According to Mark 10:41, they were "indignant" at the request of James and John. They, too, were viewing greatness and prominence in God's kingdom as a win-lose situation.

[18]The countercultural values of the kingdom with respect to power can also be seen in the experience of Paul. Our culture equates power with strength—physical, financial, emotional and relational. If power is the pathway to success, strength is the pathway to power. But Paul learned that the ways of God are very different. God allowed Satan to afflict Paul with his unnamed, though clearly very painful, "thorn in the flesh" "to keep [him] from becoming conceited" (2 Cor 12:7). Paul pleaded with God on three occasions to take this thorn away. But God mercifully refused. For God, Paul's humility was more important than his health. And in Paul's weakness, he would come to experience God's grace in a deeper way than he ever had before. God said, "My grace is sufficient for you, for my power is made perfect in weakness" (2 Cor 12:9). Paul finally got the message. He concluded, "Therefore I will boast all the more gladly about my weaknesses, so that Christ's power may rest on me. That is why, for Christ's sake, I delight in weaknesses, in insults, in hardships, in persecutions, in difficulties. For when I am weak, then I am strong" (2 Cor 12:9-10). How different and how wonderful are the ways of God with regard to strength, power, grace and success!

Chapter 3: Success in the Eyes of God

[1]I first heard this illustration from John Piper, senior pastor of Bethlehem Baptist Church, Minneapolis.

[2]This was the call of Jesus to Simon and Andrew (Mk 1:17), to Levi (Mk 2:14) and indeed to all his disciples: "Whoever wants to be my disciple must deny themselves and take up their cross and follow me" (Mk 8:34).

[3]Ronald Allen suggests that Moses' lack of faith was also exhibited in the anger with which he spoke to the people and struck the rock. He says that Moses became so angry he felt he needed to exercise wrath against the people himself rather than being willing to trust God's promise: "It is mine to avenge; I will repay" (Deut 32:35; see also Rom 12:19). Psalm 106:32-33 also speaks of the rash words of Moses as an act of disobedience: "By the waters of Meribah they angered the LORD, and trouble came to Moses because of them; for they rebelled against the Spirit of God, and rash words came from Moses' lips" ("Numbers," *Expositor's Bible Commentary*, vol. 12 [Grand Rapids: Zondervan, 1990], pp. 868-69).

[4]Kent and Barbara Hughes discuss faithfulness as a crucial component of success in God's eyes in their *Liberating Ministry from the Success Syndrome* (Wheaton,

Ill.: Crossway, 2008), pp. 35-43. They also consider other biblical criteria for success, including love (love for God with all of one's being and love for our neighbors as ourselves, Mt 22:34-40) and servanthood (following the example of Jesus, who came not "to be served but to serve and to give his life as a ransom for many," Mk 10:45). In addition, they treat the themes of believing, prayer, holiness and attitude. Each of these forms a chapter in their effort to define success from God's perspective. Ibid., pt. 3.

[5]On the paralyzing effects of the fear of failure, see John D. Searle, "The Fear of Failure," *The Expository Times* 113, no. 9 (June 2002): 311-13. Searle cites other biblical figures who also struggled with the fear of failure, including Moses (fearing his inability to speak well, Ex 6:12), Jeremiah (fearing that he was too young and again not a good speaker, Jer 1:6) and Isaiah (fearing he was not good enough, Is 6:5). In the end, each of them did overcome his fear of failure by the grace of God.

[6]Note also the example of the Christians in Macedonia, who gave generously to help their fellow believers in Jerusalem in spite of their own poverty. "In the midst of a very severe trial, their overflowing joy and their extreme poverty welled up in rich generosity" (2 Cor 8:2). Paul held them up as a model for all believers of faithful and generous giving.

[7]The pursuit of justice is clearly part of faithfulness to the character and commands of God. Among many texts in Scripture, consider Micah's statement "[God] has shown all you people what is good. And what does the LORD require of you? To act justly and to love mercy and to walk humbly with your God" (Mic 6:8).

[8]Clearly our faithfulness to God, love, servanthood and humility will evidence themselves in our outward actions and relationships. But these realities begin first and foremost in the heart. "Good people bring good things out of the good stored up in their heart, and evil people bring evil things out of the evil stored up in their heart. For out of the overflow of the heart, the mouth speaks" (Lk 6:45).

[9]This theme will be explored more fully in chapter five.

[10]Another Pauline metaphor also speaks to the need for faithfulness: being an ambassador of Christ (2 Cor 5:20). Ambassadors represent their home government to another government. They are not at liberty to act and speak however they want. They are bound by the obligation to be faithful to the wishes, desires, positions and goals of the home government. Only then will an ambassador be successful. Therefore, when Paul described himself as an ambassador of Christ, he was speaking of the need to be faithful to the goals and desires and the message of the one who sent him. The principle is true not only for those who are in vocational ministry. All who belong to Christ are sent to rep-

resent him in the world in whatever God calls them to. And that requires that they be faithful.

[11]Failing to remember this can be very unsettling spiritually. Such was the experience of Asaph, the author of Psalm 73. In this psalm, he recounted his struggles over the prosperity of the wicked (Ps 73:2-3). It seemed to go against all the covenant promises of God and caused Asaph to wonder whether his efforts to fear God and remain faithful to him were all in vain (Ps 73:13). But the resolution to Asaph's crisis of faith in this psalm involved the issue of timing: "When I tried to understand all this, it troubled me deeply till I entered the sanctuary of God; then I understood their final destiny" (Ps 73:16-17). In other words, God enabled Asaph to see that his initial observations of the relative quality of the life of the wicked and the righteous did not take into account the final score. Yes, the wicked were ahead (or so it seemed) at the end of the fifth inning. But when the final score is tallied, things will be very different. The wicked will experience the judgment of God on their wicked lifestyles— perhaps at some later point in this life but certainly in the final judgment (Ps 73:18-19). And the destiny of Asaph and all those who seek to follow God is to experience the goodness of God in full measure. This conclusion is stated at the beginning of the psalm: "Surely God is good to Israel, to those who are pure in heart." But the fullness of the goodness of God, his reward for "successfully" following him, is experienced only when the final score is counted.

[12]Many have argued against the assertion that these verses teach that faith is a gift from God. They notice, rightly, that the *this* of Ephesians 2:8 is a neuter pronoun in Greek, while *faith* is feminine. And so, they argue, faith is not included in what Paul is referring to as a gift from God. My sense, however, is that the neuter *this* is referring to the entire expression (and the entire reality) of salvation by grace through faith. All of it, in all of its dimensions, is a gift from God. This includes our faith.

[13]The U.S. Census Bureau reported in 2002, "About 50% of first marriages for men under age 45 may end in divorce, and between 44 and 52% of women's first marriages may end in divorce for these age groups" (Rose M. Kreider and Jason M. Fields, "Number, Timing, and Duration of Marriages and Divorces: 1996," U.S. Census Bureau Current Population Reports, February 2002, p. 18, cited in <www.divorcereform.org/rates.html>, part three "Projection/Prediction").

[14]Lincoln ran for the Illinois House of Representatives and lost in 1832. He subsequently won four terms in 1834, 1836, 1838 and 1840. He sought the nomination of the Whig party for the U.S. House of Representatives in 1844 but was not selected. He did win election to the U.S. House in 1846 but served only one term. He ran for the U.S. Senate in 1854 and 1858 and was defeated by Lyman Trumball and Stephen Douglas, respectively. David Herbert Don-

ald, *Lincoln* (New York: Simon & Schuster, 1995), pp. 46, 53, 60, 78-80, 114, 178-85, 196-229.

Chapter 4: Experiencing Failure

[1]This is true, even if we prefer to call these realities "mistakes" instead of "failures." See Jean M. Blomquist, "On Having Faith—*In* Failure," *Weavings* 7 (January-February 1992): 9.

[2]Jay M. Hanke, "Failure: Where the Fabric Is Torn," *Weavings* 7 (January-February 1992): 25.

[3]Blomquist, "On Having Faith," p. 8.

[4]Robert G. Kemper, "The Forced Termination," in *Mastering Transitions*, ed. Edward B. Batcher, Robert G. Kemper and Douglas Scott (Portland: Multnomah, 1991), p. 74.

[5]For the details of Madoff's Ponzi scheme, see <www.forbes.com/2008/12/12/madoff-ponzi-hedge-pf-ii-in_rl_1212croesus_inl.html>.

[6]See <http://online.wsj.com/article/SB124604151653862301.html>.

[7]Ibid. Further evidence of the lack of relational support that Madoff experienced comes from Judge Chin at his sentencing. He commented that he had not received any mitigating letters from Madoff's friends or family testifying to his good deeds. Judge Chin said, "The absence of such support is telling."

[8]See <http://bls.gov/news.release/empsit.t01.htm>. The December 2010 unemployment rate represents a drop from the 9.8 percent rate of November 2010. The rate of the previous three months was 9.6 percent.

[9]See <http://bls.gov/news.release/empsit.t12.htm>. Compare the December 2010 long-term unemployment numbers (6.4 million) with those of July 2009 (5.0 million).

[10]Media coverage of the Tiger Woods sex scandal has been ubiquitous. One clear timeline of the personal, legal, athletic and commercial impacts of the scandal can be found on ESPN Golf, "Tiger Woods Event Timeline" <http://sports.espn.go.com/golf/news/story?id=4922436>.

[11]This was not the only experience of failure as Peter followed Jesus during his earthly life. Another example involved his attempt to walk on water to come to Jesus. When he started focusing more on the wind than on Jesus, he began to sink. Jesus reached out his hand and caught him, but said to him, "You of little faith, why did you doubt?" (Mt 14:28-31).

[12]Jesus' prediction of Peter's denial is found in Matthew 26:31-35; Mark 14:27-31; Luke 22:3-34; and John 13:36-38. Peter's threefold denial is recorded in Matthew 26:69-75; Mark 14:66-72; Luke 22:55-62; and John 18:16-18, 25-27.

[13]In 2001, the evangelical ministry journal *Leadership* published the results of a survey about pastors and Internet pornography. The survey asked pastors who

had access to the Internet, "Have you ever visited a pornographic website?" Fifty-seven percent said, "Never"; 7 percent said, "More than a year ago"; 9 percent said, "Once in the past year"; 21 percent said, "A few times a year"; and 6 percent said, "A couple of times a month or more." A total of 37 percent of these pastors admitted that Internet pornography was a current temptation for them ("Pastors Viewing Internet Pornography: How Widespread Is It?" *Leadership* 22, no. 1 [Winter 2001]: 93).

[14]The classical understanding of specific temptations attacking those involved in church leadership is the trio of money, sex and power. See Richard Foster's *Money, Sex, and Power: The Challenge of the Disciplined Life* (San Francisco: Harper and Row, 1985), which goes beyond just specific pastoral temptations in these areas. It is a realistic and helpful treatment for all Christians.

[15]Michael O. Emerson and Christian Smith, *Divided by Faith: Evangelical Faith and the Problem of Race in America* (New York: Oxford University Press, 2001).

[16]Philip Yancey, *What's So Amazing About Grace?* (Grand Rapids: Zondervan, 1997), p. 130.

[17]Ibid., p. 133.

[18]J. K. Rowling, "The Fringe Benefits of Failure, and the Importance of Imagination," *Harvard Magazine*, June 5, 2008 <http://harvardmagazine.com/commence ment/the-fringe-benefits-failure-the-importance-imagination?sms_ss+email &at_xt+4d23951f2c1221ae%CO#>.

[19]"Clooney's Sexy Sour Grapes," *Chicago Tribune*, November 26, 2008, "Live!" section, p. 2.

[20]Scot McKnight cites the following references from the Gospel of Mark to substantiate this consistent pattern of failure on the part of the disciples: they failed on several occasions to understand Jesus' teaching (Mk 4:10, 13, 33-34; 7:17-19; 8:16-21); they experienced fear rather than faith in the boat with Jesus in the storm (Mk 4:35-41); they were blind as to Jesus' ability to provide for them (Mk 6:35-37, 43; 8:4); they were unwilling and unable to accept Gentiles and children (Mk 9:14-19); they were unable to trust God to heal (Mk 9:14-19); they yearned for the most valuable status among the apostles (Mk 10:35-45); and they were unwilling to support Jesus in his passion (Mk 14:37, 40, 54, 66-72) (*The Jesus Creed: Loving God, Loving Others* [Brewster, Mass.: Paraclete Press, 2004], p. 323).

[21]Ibid., pp. 211-12. The New Testament is clear that sinless perfection is not something Christians will experience in this life (Mt 6:12; Phil 3:12-14; 1 Jn 1:8-10). I will explore this further in chapter six.

[22]See Erwin Lutzer, *Failure: The Back Door to Success* (Chicago: Moody Press, 1975), p. 44.

[23]Lewis Smedes, *Forgive and Forget* (San Francisco: Harper & Row, 1984), p. 71.

[24]Brainy Quote, "Albert Einstein Quotes" <www.brainyquote.com/quotes/quotes /a/alberteins133991.html>.

[25]After hearing Peter's report of how Cornelius and his family had responded to the gospel of Christ when Peter had proclaimed it to them, the apostles in Jerusalem exclaim, "So then, even to Gentiles God has granted repentance that leads to life" (Acts 11:18). This is true not only at the beginning of one's Christian life but throughout. On repentance as a gift of God's grace, see also 2 Timothy 2:25-26.

[26]Peter Scazerro labels three ineffective and unproductive ways to deal with the pain and hardship of failures. Using the metaphor of the thorns and thistles that emerged in the Garden of Eden as a result of God's curse following the sin of Adam and Eve, Scazerro says that rather than being broken and humbled by the thorns and thistles of life, we tend to either flee from them (seeking to anesthetize the pain by burying it in an addictive behavior), fight them (becoming angry, bitter and/or violent because we feel life is not going our way) or hide them (living in ways that cover up how damaged, limited and imperfect we are) (*The Emotionally Healthy Church: A Strategy for Discipleship That Actually Changes Lives* [Grand Rapids: Zondervan, 2003], p. 113).

Chapter 5: Grappling with Failure Theologically

[1]The life-changing impact of having one's life centered on and shaped by the Word of God can be seen in Psalm 1. This psalm opens with a sharp contrast between two kinds of people: the righteous, who are blessed by God, and the wicked, who are not (Ps 1:1-3, 4-5). The righteous "do not walk in step with the wicked or stand in the way that sinners take or sit in the company of mockers." Rather, they "delight in the law of the LORD and meditate on his law day and night." The outcome of this kind of life is described in powerful and hope-giving imagery: "They are like a tree planted by streams of water, which yields its fruit in season and whose leaf does not wither—whatever they do prospers." Who among us does not long for that kind of vibrant and fruitful life—especially after we have failed?

[2]A very helpful treatment of the image of God as both status and standard, and the implications this has for human dignity, can be found in C. Ben Mitchell et al., *Biotechnology and the Human Good* (Washington, D.C.: Georgetown University Press, 2007), pp. 68-76.

[3]As humans, we have a hard enough time remembering the past, even the fairly recent past. Our knowledge of the present is limited by our social and temporal location. And our knowledge of the future consists of predictions and forecasts that all too often go astray. What a sharp contrast to the infinite perfection of God's knowledge. He "knows everything" (1 Jn 3:20). The extent of God's

knowledge of the future, particularly his foreknowledge of human decisions, has been much debated within certain circles of evangelical theology. For an extended argument for the universality of God's foreknowledge, see Steven C. Roy, *How Much Does God Foreknow? A Comprehensive Biblical Study* (Downers Grove, Ill.: InterVarsity Press, 2006).

[4]See Millard J. Erickson, *Christian Theology*, 2nd ed. (Grand Rapids: Baker, 1998), p. 515.

[5]Shame is a broader category of emotional response than guilt. It may accompany guilt over moral wrongdoing, but it may also be felt in cases like this, in which there is no moral guilt. For helpful introductions to these issues, see Lewis Smedes, *Shame and Grace* (San Francisco: HarperCollins, 1993); and Becca Cowan Johnson, *Good Guilt, Bad Guilt* (Downers Grove, Ill.: InterVarsity Press, 1996).

[6]Jean M. Blomquist, "On Having Faith—*In* Failure," *Weavings*, January-February 1992, p. 14.

[7]Consider the teaching of James about how our inherently limited knowledge of the future should humble us and keep us from boasting: "Now listen, you who say, 'Today or tomorrow we will go to this or that city, spend a year there, carry on business and make money.' *Why, you do not even know what will happen tomorrow. What is your life?* You are a mist that appears for a little while and then vanishes. Instead, you ought to say, 'If it is the Lord's will, we will live and do this or that.' As it is, you boast in your arrogant schemes. All such boasting is evil" (Jas 4:13-16, emphasis added).

[8]Other examples of the reality of risk and the rightness of taking risks for the cause of God can be found in Scripture. Consider, for example, the actions of Joab, the commander of the armies of Israel. In 2 Samuel 10, the Israelites found themselves surrounded by two enemies: the Ammonites and the Arameans. In response, Joab divided his troops. He put his brother Abishai in charge of one group and took command of the other himself. Both brothers pledged to help each other, and Joab said, "Be strong and let us fight bravely for our people and the cities of our God. The LORD will do what is good in his sight" (2 Sam 10:12). In other words, Joab made a strategic decision in defense of the cities of God, not knowing for sure how it would turn out. There was risk in his decision to fight in this way (and risk in a decision to flee as well). But Joab made his decision and turned the results over to God, saying "The LORD will do what is good in his sight." See also the response of Shadrach, Meshach and Abednego to Nebuchadnezzar in Daniel 3:16-18.

[9]Unwillingness to take risks can lead us to refuse to step out in faith and follow God's direction. Such was the case with the nation of Israel in Numbers 13–14. Moses sent twelve spies to explore the Promised Land. When they returned,

ten of the twelve spies reported that the inhabitants of the land were too big and too powerful for the Israelites to conquer. Even though two of the spies, Caleb and Joshua, sought to encourage the people to trust God to fulfill his promises and bring them into the land, the people refused to go. Their unwillingness to take risks was wrong in God's eyes, and the people wandered in the wilderness for forty years because of it.

[10]Blomquist, "On Having Faith," p. 11.

[11]The explicit statement of Genesis 1 that both male and female are equally created in the image of God is crucial for self-acceptance of our gender. It is also filled with deep and profound implications for the way God would want both genders to relate to each other.

[12]In our fallen world, there are some conditions (birth defects, genetic diseases and so on) that raise very difficult questions about the role of God the Creator. Yet in Scripture, God says that he is involved even in the most difficult of human conditions, working out his wise and holy and loving purposes. For example, after Moses said that he could not obey God's call to go to Pharaoh to deliver the Israelites from bondage because of difficulties in his speech, God responded, "Who gave human beings their mouths? Who makes them deaf or mute? Who gives them sight or makes them blind? Is it not I, the LORD?" (Ex 4:11-12). While, no doubt, there remain many unanswered questions in situations like these, a thankful, trusting response is to be preferred far more than the kind of bitter accusation referred to by Paul: "Shall what is formed say to the one who formed it, 'Why did you make me like this?'" (Rom 9:20). Paul raised this rhetorical question in the context of discussing God's election and objections that might be raised against this reality. But the concept has a much wider application. In the Old Testament background to this question, Isaiah affirmed that the pot questioning the wisdom and skill of the potter (telling the potter, "you know nothing") is a case of "[turning] things upside down" (Is 29:16).

[13]On the need for us to accept ourselves the way God has made us, see Erwin W. Lutzer, Failure: The Back Door to Success (Chicago: Moody Press, 1975), pp. 72-75.

[14]On this important form of discernment, see Blomquist, "On Having Faith," p. 13.

[15]Stephen Seamands quoted the perceptive words of Carl Jung in this regard: "The acceptance of oneself is the essence of the whole moral problem and the epitome of a whole outlook on life. That I feed the hungry, that I forgive an insult, that I love my enemy in the name of Christ—all these are undoubtedly great virtues. What I do unto the least of my brethren, that I do unto Christ. But what if I should discover that the least amongst them all, the poorest of all

the beggars, the most impudent of all the offenders, the very enemy himself—
that these are within me, and that I myself stand in need of the alms of my
own kindness—that I myself am the enemy who must be loved—what then?
As a rule, the Christian's attitude is then reversed; there is no longer any question of love or long-suffering; we say to the brother within us 'Raca,' and condemn and rage against ourselves." Seamands's conclusion, based on his theological reflection and ministry experience is that "we often find it much easier
to extend grace to others than to ourselves" (*Ministry in the Image of God: The
Trinitarian Shape of Christian Service* [Downers Grove, Ill.: InterVarsity Press,
2005], pp. 125-26).

[16]James Denny once said, "Of all human experiences, the most universal is a bad
conscience" (quoted in J. I. Packer, *God's Words: Studies of Key Bible Themes*
[Downers Grove, Ill.: InterVarsity Press, 1981], p. 201). Other biblical testimo-
nies to the universality of sin throughout humanity include 1 Kings 8:46
("There is no one who does not sin"); Psalm 143:1-2 ("O LORD, listen to my
prayer. . . . Do not bring your servant into judgment, for no one living is righteous before you"); Ecclesiastes 7:20 ("There is no one on earth who is righteous, no one who does what is right and never sins"); and Romans 3:9-10 ("We
have already made the charge that Jews and Gentiles alike are all under sin. As
it is written, 'There is no one righteous, not even one'").

[17]See Lutzer, *Failure*, p. 42.

[18]In Exodus 34:5, we read that the Lord came down to Moses while he was on
Mount Sinai and "proclaimed his name, the LORD [Hebrew *Yahweh*]" to him.
The "name" of God signifies his character and his essential nature. What follows in Exodus 3:6-7 is an elaboration of the covenant name of Yahweh. God's
self-description of himself as a compassionate, gracious, forgiving God clari-
fies our understanding of the very heart of the nature of God himself.

[19]Jesus told a series of three parables that deal with the reality of "lostness" and
the joy that comes when what was lost is found: a shepherd rejoicing over the
finding of a lost sheep (Lk 15:1-7), a woman rejoicing when she found a lost
coin (Lk 15:8-9) and a father who rejoices when his lost son is "found" (Lk
15:11-32). The common theme of rejoicing certainly points to the great joy God
experiences when his lost children are reconciled to himself and are "found."

[20]The language of justification is used in the Old Testament in legal contexts to
describe the actions of judges adjudicating judicial cases. See, for example,
Deuteronomy 25:1 ("When people have a dispute, they are to take it to court
and the judges will decide the case, acquitting [justifying] the innocent and
condemning the guilty") and Proverbs 17:15 ("Acquitting [justifying] the guilty
and condemning the innocent—the LORD detests them both"). In addition, we
find in the New Testament the language of justification in opposition to con-

demnation, which is clearly a legal verdict. See Romans 8:33-34 ("Who will bring any charge against those whom God has chosen? It is God who justifies. Who then can condemn?"). These texts form a strong argument for a judicial, forensic understanding of justification as opposed to the traditional Roman Catholic understanding of justification that is primarily moral.

[21]During the Protestant Reformation, the nature of justification was one of the chief points of conflict between Protestants such as Martin Luther and the Roman Catholic Church of his day. Luther's view, which has been held by confessional Protestants to this day, understood the Pauline verb "to justify" to mean "to declare righteous." He understood justification to be legal or forensic, involving the imputed righteousness of Christ being credited to the account of believers. This justification is received by God's grace through faith alone (*sola fide*) at the beginning of one's Christian life. By contrast the Roman Catholic position, specifically as articulated by the Council of Trent (the official Roman Catholic response to the Protestant Reformation, 1545-1563) sees the verb "to justify" to mean "to make righteous." This view understands justification to be primarily moral, involving the righteousness of Christ being infused into his followers. This justification is received by God's grace through a combination of faith and works and is a lifelong process. Thus one can never know if he or she is justified until the final judgment. The texts listed in the previous endnote, along with texts that speak of God being justified (Lk 7:29; Rom 3:4; 1 Tim 3:16) and of people justifying themselves (Lk 10:29; 16:15) all argue for the correctness of Luther's understanding of justification as a forensic declaration of righteousness. Perhaps most persuasive of all is the structure of Paul's argument in Romans. After proclaiming the good news of justification (Rom 3:21–4:25) and describing some of its benefits (Rom 5), Paul goes on to deal with a potential objection that could be raised, writing, "What shall we say, then? Shall we go on sinning so that grace may increase?" (Rom 6:1). This objection would be unthinkable if justification was in fact primarily an act of moral transformation. But if it is a judicial declaration, the objection and Paul's response to it makes sense.

[22]In Romans 3:23-26, Paul piled up terms to describe the atoning death of Jesus Christ and its accomplishments. He spoke of the death of Christ, utilizing the language of the marketplace ("redemption"), the language of personal relationships ("sacrifice of atonement," or more literally "propitiation"), the language of Old Testament sacrifices ("shedding of his blood") and the language of the law court ("justifies"). The multiplicity of metaphors speaks loudly of the multifaceted glory of Christ's atonement.

[23]There has arisen within evangelical Christianity in recent years a debate over whether the righteousness of Christ is indeed imputed to believers. Robert

Gundry started this debate by affirming that, while our sins are imputed to Christ, his righteousness is not imputed to us (rather, in justification it is our faith that is imputed to us as righteousness). See Robert H. Gundry, "Why I Didn't Endorse 'The Gospel of Jesus Christ: An Evangelical Celebration' . . . Even Though I Wasn't Asked To," *Books and Culture* 7, no. 1 (2001): 6-9, and his response to the criticism of Thomas C. Oden: "On Oden's Answer," *Books and Culture* 7, no. 2 (2001): 14-15, 39. John Piper responded to Gundry's claims in *Counted Righteous in Christ: Should We Abandon the Imputation of Christ's Righteousness?* (Wheaton, Ill.: Crossway, 2002). Further responses to this dialogue can be found in essays by Robert H. Gundry, "The Nonimputation of Christ's Righteousness," and D. A. Carson, "The Vindication of Imputation: On Fields of Discourse and Semantic Fields," in *Justification: What's at Stake in the Current Debates*, ed. Mark Husbands and Daniel J. Treier (Downers Grove, Ill.: Inter-Varsity Press, 2004), pp. 17-45, 46-78. As I read the New Testament, the imputation of Christ's righteousness is the view most consistent with biblical evidence.

[24]Scripture is clear that the effects and consequences of our sin may remain even after our sins are forgiven. For example, after David confessed his sin of adultery with Bathsheba and of the murder of Uriah, God's forgiveness was quick in coming. The prophet Nathan spoke for God, "The LORD has taken away your sin. You are not going to die" (2 Sam 12:13). But consequences remained. Nathan continued, "But because by doing this you have shown utter contempt for the LORD, the son born to you will die" (2 Sam 12:14). Yet these consequences, for David or for any other forgiven sinner, are not the result of God's condemnation. That has been put away forever through the death of Christ. Even God's disciplinary actions are the loving work of our heavenly Father to shape us more and more into the likeness of Christ (Heb 12:5-11). Even when the consequences of our sin are not taken away, our renewed, restored relationship with God remains. His forgiveness can never be taken away.

[25]Paul spoke of reconciliation with God as the fruit of the death of Christ in Romans 5:9-10; 2 Corinthians 5:18-21; and Colossians 1:21-23. In Ephesians 2:11-22, he described the reality that those who have been reconciled to God through Christ are also reconciled to one another (even across barriers such as race, ethnicity, gender and class) in the one new humanity God is creating in Christ.

[26]Jesus had in fact predicted this falling away of his disciples: " 'You will all fall away,' Jesus told them, 'for it is written: "I will strike the shepherd and the sheep will be scattered" ' " (Mk 14:27, quoting Zech 13:7).

[27]On this monumental encounter, see Kent and Barbara Hughes, *Liberating Ministry from the Success Syndrome* (Wheaton, Ill.: Crossway, 2008), pp. 54-57.

Chapter 6: More Truths of Grace

[1]See also the statement of John the Baptist, who referred to Jesus Christ as "the Lamb of God who takes away the sins of the world" (Jn 1:29).

[2]The connection between God's holiness and our obligation as Christians to pursue holiness in our lives is beautifully expressed in 1 Peter 1:15-16: "Just as he who called you is holy, so be holy in all you do; for it is written, 'Be holy, because I am holy'" (quoting Lev 11:44-45).

[3]J. I. Packer, *Keep in Step with the Spirit* (Old Tappan, N.J.: Revell, 1984), p. 95.

[4]See Bruce Demarest, *The Cross and Salvation* (Wheaton, Ill.: Crossway, 1997), p. 407.

[5]The most common New Testament designation of Christians is "holy ones" or "saints" (for example, Rom 1:7; Eph 1:1; Phil 1:1). A fuller expression of this comes in 1 Corinthians 1:2. Paul said he was writing to "the church of God in Corinth, to those *sanctified* in Christ and called to be his *holy people*" (emphasis added). Peter said that the Christians he was writing to are "a chosen people, a royal priesthood, a holy nation, God's special possession" (1 Pet 2:9). References like these point to one crucial dimension of biblical sanctification. It is a position that all Christians occupy by the grace of God—that of having been set apart by God and for God.

[6]In addition to the texts cited above, note 2 Corinthians 7:1: "Since we have these promises, dear friends, let us purify ourselves from everything that contaminates body and spirit, perfecting holiness out of reverence for God." Thus our holiness needs to be perfected as we purify ourselves. A text that beautifully combines the positional and the process dimensions of sanctification in the lives of Christians is Hebrews 10:14. Speaking of the death of Christ and its effects, the author stated, "By one sacrifice [Christ] has made perfect [perfect tense, denoting a past act with continuing implications] forever those who are being made holy [present tense, denoting ongoing action]."

[7]Christians in the Wesleyan tradition have often appealed to John Wesley's teaching of "entire sanctification" or "Christian perfection." Wesley saw this as a powerful work of God's grace in which the Christian is permanently set free from willful, voluntary transgressions of known laws of God. But at the same time, he insisted that this does not involve "absolute" or "total" perfection. Christians are always able to fall away from the grace they have been given and under even the best of circumstances always experience imperfections as part and parcel of living in a fallen world. Thus even after experiencing Christian perfection, Christians still need to pray for forgiveness as instructed in the Lord's Prayer, and they are still obligated to grow in grace. See John Wesley, *A Plain Account of Christian Perfection* (London: Epworth, 1968); and the summary of a Wesleyan view of sanctification by Melvin E. Dieter, "The Wesleyan

View," in *Five Views of Sanctification,* ed. Stanley N. Gundry (Grand Rapids: Zondervan, 1987), pp. 11-46. This entire book is a helpful description of various approaches Christians have taken to understanding sanctification.

[8]An additional biblical text that reinforces the lifelong, never fully completed process of sanctification is Philippians 3:12, in which Paul described his own process of growth toward becoming fully like Christ: "Not that I have already obtained all this, or have already become perfect, but I press on to take hold of that for which Christ Jesus took hold of me." Admittedly, Paul was talking about his own experience. But if he is not perfect, who among us could be? Other texts that reinforce this truth include James 3:2 and 5:16.

[9]For example, Jesus commanded his followers, "Be perfect, therefore, as your heavenly Father is perfect" (Mt 5:48). And note once again the command from Peter cited above (n. 2): "Just as he who called you is holy, so be holy in all you do; for it is written: 'Be holy, because I am holy'" (1 Pet 1:15-16).

[10]On the "negative" side of the Spirit's work of transformation (leading us to say no to sin), Paul wrote that it is "by the Spirit" that Christians are to "put to death the misdeeds of the body" (Rom 8:13). On the positive side, consider the beautiful picture of the virtues of Christlikeness that the Spirit produces in the children of God. Paul described the "fruit of the Spirit" as "love, joy, peace, patience, kindness, goodness, faithfulness, gentleness and self-control" (Gal 5:22-23). In designating these virtues as "the fruit of the Spirit," he was clearly saying that their ultimate source is the Spirit of God and not our own unaided efforts. But in this very context, Paul instructed his readers—in order to pursue this fruit—to "walk by the Spirit," by "[being] led by the Spirit" and by "[keeping] in step with the Spirit" (Gal 5:16, 18, 25). Paul was clear that the ultimate divine agency in producing this kind of character does not remove the responsibility of Christians to pursue it.

[11]The implications of the causal particle *for* (*gar* in Greek) at the beginning of Philippians 2:13 must not be overlooked. This word establishes the causal connection that Paul was trying to make. It is only because of the inner work of God that Christians can and must live out their salvation in their personal and corporate lives.

[12]The intensity of effort in the pursuit of moral transformation can be seen in 2 Peter 1:5-7: "For this reason, *make every effort* to add to your faith goodness; and to goodness, knowledge; and to knowledge, self-control; and to self-control, perseverance; and to perseverance, godliness; and to godliness, mutual affection; and to mutual affection, love" (emphasis added). The beginning phrase, "for this reason," points back to the preceding verses, which speak of God's work on our behalf—providing us through his power with "everything we need for a godly life" and giving us "his very great and precious promises so

that through them you may participate in the divine nature" (2 Pet 1:3-4). Again we see that it is God's work for us that encourages us and motivates us to diligent and ultimately productive moral effort.

[13]Especially significant is the promise of 1 Corinthians 10:13, "No temptation has overtaken you except what is common to us all. And God is faithful; he will not let you be tempted beyond what you can bear. But when you are tempted, he will also provide a way out so that you can endure it." Nothing in this section about the inevitability of our lifelong struggle with sin should be taken to deny that it is possible to resist the temptations to sin that we encounter.

[14]This ongoing tension in our lives as followers of Christ is the thesis of Peter K. Nelson, *Spiritual Formation: Ever Forming, Never Formed* (Colorado Springs: Biblica Publishing, 2010).

[15]Those wanting to follow AA's twelve steps to recover from addiction must admit that they were and are powerless over alcohol and that their lives have become unmanageable (step one) and that only a Power greater than themselves could restore them (step two). They must be willing to make a searching and fearless moral inventory of themselves (step four). And having done that, they must admit to God, to themselves and to another human being the exact nature of their wrongs (step five). See "The Twelve Steps of Alcoholics Anonymous," Alcoholics Anonymous <www.aa.org/en_pdfs/smf-121_en.pdf> (accessed December 16, 2008).

[16]The honest and open sharing of successes and struggles that characterizes AA groups does not lead to despairing pessimism; a characteristic of AA is its optimism. If one really does stick to the twelve steps, there is the confident hope of living in sobriety.

[17]Stephen Seamands, *Ministry in the Image of God: The Trinitarian Shape of Christian Service* (Downers Grove, Ill.: InterVarsity Press, 2005), p. 85.

[18]Jean Blomquist, "On Having Faith—*In* Failure," *Weavings*, January-February 1992, p. 14.

[19]Today's New International Version notes that the Greek word translated "adoption to sonship" (*huiothesia*) is "a legal term referring to the full legal standing of an adopted male heir in Roman culture" (footnote to Eph 1:5). This exalted status belongs to all children of God, both male and female, as Paul argued in Galatians 3:26-29, where he clearly stated that both male and female believers are equally God's children and heirs according to his promise. But it is striking for Paul to use this admittedly patriarchial language to describe the highly loved and honored status that God grants to all his children.

[20]J. I. Packer, *Knowing God* (Downers Grove, Ill.: InterVarsity Press, 1993), p. 207.

[21]When Scripture speaks of God as our father, it is speaking metaphorically, using a more familiar concept (a father) to describe something less familiar (God in his relationship to us). The Bible is filled with a multitude of meta-

phorical expressions that describe God (God as shepherd, king, judge, lover, warrior and so on), but in no case are the realities being compared identical. We must remember that, in the words of Sallie McFague, every metaphor contains within itself "the whisper, 'It is and it is not'" (*Metaphorical Theology: Models of God in Religious Language* [Philadelphia: Fortress, 1982], p. 13). So when we consider metaphors used to describe God, we must always consider both similarities and differences that exist between the earthly reality and its divine referent. This means that when we speak of God as a father, we must pay attention both to the ways in which God is like our fathers and ways in which he is unlike them.

[22]Packer is worth quoting at length at this point. "The thought of our Maker becoming our perfect parent—faithful in love and care, generous and thoughtful, interested in all we do, respecting our individuality, skillful in training us, wise in guidance, always available, helping us to find ourselves in maturity, integrity, and uprightness—is a thought which can have meaning for everybody, whether we come to it by saying, 'I had a wonderful father, and I see that God is like that, only more so,' or by saying, 'My father disappointed me here, and here, and here, but God, praise his name, will be very different,' or even by saying, 'I have never known what it means to have a father on earth, but thank God now I have one in heaven.' The truth is that all of us have a positive ideal of fatherhood by which we judge our own and others' fathers" (*Knowing God*, p. 204).

[23]Before God is the father of believers, he is first and foremost "the God and Father of our Lord Jesus Christ" (Eph 1:3). Jesus Christ is God's one and only Son eternally and by nature. Those who believe in Jesus are God's children by adoption.

[24]See, for example, Jesus' statements in John 4:34, "My food is to do the will of him who sent me and to finish his work"; John 5:19, "The Son can do nothing by himself; he can do only what he sees his Father doing, because whatever the Father does the Son also does"; John 6:38, "I have come down from heaven not to do my will but to do the will of him who sent me"; and John 17:4, "I have brought you [Father] glory on earth by finishing the work you gave me to do."

[25]See Jesus' statements about the Father's love for him in John 5:20, "For the Father loves the Son and shows him all he does," and John 15:9-10, "As the Father has loved me, so have I loved you. Now remain in my love. If you keep my commands, you will remain in my love, just as I have kept my Father's commands and remain in his love." See also Jesus' prayer to the Father on behalf of his followers: "I in them and you in me—so that they may be brought to complete unity. Then the world will know that you sent me and have loved them even as you have loved me. Father, I want those you have given me to be with me where I am, and to see my glory, the glory you have given me because you loved me before the creation of the world" (Jn 17:23-24).

[26]John described Jesus, the one and only Son of God, as the one "who is himself God and is in closest relationship with the Father" (Jn 1:18). The Father's relational presence and intimacy with his Son is indicated through the words of Jesus in John 8:29, "The one who sent me is with me; he has not left me alone, for I always do what pleases him," and John 16:32, "A time is coming and in fact has come when you will be scattered, each to your own home. You will leave me all alone. Yet I am not alone, for my Father is with me."

[27]The Father's purpose is indicated in John 5:22-23: "The Father judges no one, but has entrusted all judgment to the Son, that all may honor the Son." This is what Jesus prayed for in John 17:1: "Father, the hour has come. Glorify your Son, that your Son may glorify you." Stephen Seamands delineates a similar set of four characteristics that describe the intratrinitarian relationships between Father, Son and Holy Spirit (both in eternity and during the earthly life of Jesus): full equality, glad submission, joyful intimacy and mutual deference. He also looks to the Gospel of John to see them expressed (*Ministry in the Image of God*, pp. 35-38).

[28]On this parable, see Henri J. M. Nouwen, *The Return of the Prodigal Son: A Story of Homecoming* (New York: Image, 1992).

[29]This parable is the third of a series of three parables in Luke 15. Luke introduced them by noting that the tax collectors and sinners were gathering around Jesus to hear him. But the Pharisees and teachers of the law muttered against Jesus, criticizing him for welcoming sinners and eating with them (Lk 15:1-2). In other words, Jesus was not acting like a man of God would. They believed that God was so holy that he would always and only separate himself from sinners. So, they concluded, if Jesus was really sent from God, he would do the same thing. To correct this misperception, Jesus told these three parables, saying, in essence, "I'll tell you what God is really like. He is like a shepherd who seeks after a lost sheep; he is like a woman who searches for a lost coin; and he is like a father who loves and seeks both of his lost sons." This context makes it clear that though both sons are important characters, Jesus' primary focus is on the father.

[30]Henri Nouwen quotes the penetrating explanation of Kenneth Bailey: "For over fifteen years I have been asking people of all walks of life from Morocco to India and from Turkey to the Sudan about the implications of a son's request for his inheritance while his father is still living. The answer has already been emphatically the same . . . the conversation runs as follows, Has anyone ever made such a request in your village? Never! Could anyone make such a request? Impossible! If anyone ever did, what would happen? His father would beat him, of course! Why? The request means—he wants his father to die." In addition, the younger son in the parable asks for the right to dispose of his part

of the inheritance. "After signing over his possessions to his son, the father still has the right to live off the proceeds . . . as long as he is alive. Here the younger son gets, and thus is assumed to have demanded, disposition to which, even more explicitly, he has no right until the death of his father. The implication of 'Father, I cannot wait for you to die' underlies both requests" (*The Return of the Prodigal Son: A Story of Homecoming*, pp. 35-36).

[31]Tim Keller, "The Advent of Humility," *Christianity Today*, December 2008, p. 52.

[32]The grammar of Paul's statement is unusual. The subject of 2 Corinthians 4:17 is "our light and momentary troubles." Paul stated that *they* are achieving this eternal glory. Now, in light of Paul's broader theology, it is clear that God is the ultimate agent, working through our light and momentary troubles to achieve the eternal glory he is preparing for all his children. Apart from God's gracious and powerful work, suffering can actually achieve the opposite.

[33]J. K. Rowling, "The Fringe Benefits of Failure, and the Importance of Imagination," *The Harvard Magazine*, June 5, 2008 <http://harvardmagazine.com/commencement/the-fringe-benefits-failure-the-importance-imagination?sms_ss+email&at_xt+4d23951f2c1221ae%CO#>.

[34]Blomquist, "On Having Faith," p. 12. Her use of the word *may* is best understood, I think, in terms of our present, subjective experience. Here and now, as we grapple with failure, we "may" come into the light as a result. And the reality is that there are times when suffering and failure may lead us to close our minds and hearts to what God wants to do. But for the children of God, 2 Corinthians 4:17 would lead us to substitute the verb *will* for the verb *may*.

[35]The experience of the apostle Paul confirms this truth. Prior to his conversion to faith in Christ, he was a persecutor of Christ and his followers. His sense of guilt over these sinful failures was great—he called himself "the worst of sinners" (1 Tim 1:16). But his experience of God's overwhelming grace in Christ magnified the saving purpose of God and his magnificent patience. This had a huge impact on Paul himself and on those who saw his transformation. Such was his testimony: "Here is a trustworthy saying that deserves full acceptance: Christ Jesus came into the world to save sinners—of whom I am the worst. But for that very reason I was shown mercy so that in me, the worst of sinners, Christ Jesus might display his immense patience as an example for those who would believe in him and receive eternal life" (1 Tim 1:15-16).

[36]Jesus' death on the cross, which provides forgiveness for our sins, also triumphs over all the powers of evil. Paul linked these two concepts in Colossians 2:13-15: "He forgave us all our sins, having canceled the charge of our legal indebtedness, which stood against us and condemned us; he has taken it away, nailing it to the cross. And having disarmed the powers and authorities, he made a public spectacle of them, triumphing over them by the cross."

Chapter 7: Responding to Failure

[1]John Gardner, "Rewind Your Clock," Stanford Alumni Association <http://alumni.gsb.stanford.edu/lifelonglearning/research_ideas/human_resources_gardner2.html>.

[2]Jesus said that the greatest and most important commandment of all is, "Love the Lord your God with all your heart and with all your soul and with all your mind and with all your strength" (Mk 12:30). In other words, we are to love God with our whole being. One key implication is that while knowledge of God and all he has revealed to us is a crucial part of a relationship with God (we are to love him "with all [our] mind"), it is not enough. We are also to love God with all our heart, soul and strength.

[3]When we twenty-first-century North Americans speak of head and heart, we are almost always distinguishing our cognitive thoughts (head) from our emotions (heart). But when the Bible speaks of the heart, no such distinction is in mind. In the Bible, the heart refers to the deepest center and core of the human person. It includes thoughts, emotions and volitions, all functioning together in interconnected ways. For a helpful discussion of how this biblical view of the heart plays out in the lives of contemporary people, see Dallas Willard, *Renovation of the Heart: Putting On the Character of Christ* (Colorado Springs: NavPress, 2002), especially chapter two, "The Heart in the System of Life."

[4]The literature on spiritual disciplines is large and growing. For helpful introductions, see Richard Foster, *Celebration of Discipline: The Path to Spiritual Growth* (San Francisco: Harper & Row, 1978); Dallas Willard, *The Spirit of the Disciplines: Understanding How God Changes Lives* (San Francisco: Harper & Row, 1988); and Donald S. Whitney, *Spiritual Disciplines for the Christian Life* (Colorado Springs: NavPress, 1991).

[5]Henri Nouwen, *Making All Things New: An Invitation to the Spiritual Life* (San Francisco: HarperSanFrancisco, 1981), p. 68, quoted in Tony Campolo and Mary Albert Darling, *The God of Intimacy and Action: Reconnecting Ancient Spiritual Practices, Evangelism, and Justice* (San Francisco: Jossey-Bass, 2007), p. 77.

[6]Willard, *Spirit of the Disciplines*, p. ix, emphasis in original.

[7]Willard provides an introductory list of spiritual disciplines divided into two categories: disciplines of abstinence and disciplines of engagement. Among the disciplines of abstinence, he includes solitude, silence, fasting, frugality, chastity, secrecy and sacrifice. Among the disciplines of engagement, he includes study, worship, celebration, service, prayer, fellowship, confession and submission (ibid., pp. 158-90).

[8]Campolo and Darling, *God of Intimacy*, p. 77.

[9]J. I. Packer said we must "turn each truth we learn *about* God into matter for meditation *before* God, leading to prayer and praise *to* God." He then defined

meditation as "the activity of calling to mind, and thinking over, and dwelling on, and applying to oneself, the various things that one knows about the works and ways and purposes and promises of God. It is an activity of holy thought, consciously performed in the presence of God, under the eye of God, by the help of God, as a means of communion with God. Its purpose is to clear one's mental and spiritual vision of God, and to let His truth make its full and proper impact on one's mind and heart" (*Knowing God* [Downers Grove, Ill.: Inter-Varsity Press, 1993], pp. 18-19).

[10]Believing that God has something very personal to say to us through his Word, Demarest says that we are to "prayerfully ponder, muse, and 'chew' the words of Scripture." The goal of such meditation is "to permit the Holy Spirit to activate the life-giving Word of God so that something more of our lives is transformed to bring us, every day, a little closer to the image of Christ" (*Satisfy Your Soul: Restoring the Heart of Christian Spirituality* [Colorado Springs: NavPress, 1999], p. 133).

[11]An ancient form of this kind of meditation is called *lectio divina* ("sacred reading"). For a brief but helpful introduction to this practice, see Demarest, *Satisfy Your Soul*, pp. 135-37. This form of meditation has also been called "formative reading." See Mel Lawrenz, *The Dynamics of Spiritual Formation* (Grand Rapids: Baker, 2000), pp. 56-66.

[12]Quoted by Haddon Robinson in the foreword to Aubrey Malphurs, *Developing a Vision for Ministry in the 21st Century* (Grand Rapids: Baker, 1999), p. 10.

[13]Crawford W. Loritts Jr., *Leadership as an Identity: The Four Traits of Those Who Wield Lasting Influence* (Chicago: Moody Press, 2009), p. 96.

[14]Professor John Gardner encourages lifelong learning from all the experiences of life: "Learn from your failures. Learn from your successes. When you hit a spell of trouble ask, 'What is it trying to teach me?' The lessons aren't always happy ones, but they keep coming" ("Rewind Your Clock," p. 1).

[15]For example, Jesus said, "Ask and it will be given to you; seek and you will find; knock and the door will be opened to you. For everyone who asks receives; those who seek find; and to those who knock, the door will be opened" (Mt 7:7-8). And Paul said, "Do not be anxious about anything, but in every situation, by prayer and petition, with thanksgiving, present your requests to God. And the peace of God, which transcends all understanding, will guard your hearts and minds in Christ Jesus" (Phil 4:6-7).

[16]Jesus said, "If two of you on earth agree about anything you ask for, it will be done for you by my Father in heaven. For where two or three come together in my name, there I am with them" (Mt 18:19-20). And James said, in the context of praying for those who are sick, "Confess your sins to each other and pray for each other so that you may be healed. The prayer of a righteous person is powerful and effective" (Jas 5:16).

[17]Quoted by Kent and Barbara Hughes, *Liberating Ministry from the Success Syndrome* (Wheaton, Ill.: Crossway, 2008), p. 72.

[18]The Hugheses liken our lives to a photographic plate and prayer to a time exposure to God. As we expose ourselves to God's presence in prayer, "his image is imprinted more and more upon us. More and more we absorb the image of his character, his love, his wisdom, his way of dealing with life and people" (ibid., pp. 72-73). Specifically with regard to our failures, John Navonne writes, "Failure, whether culpable or non-culpable, can always be redeemed into a kind of *felix culpa* ["happy fall"] through the transforming power of love. This is the lesson of the cross, where the very symbol of failure and death has been transformed into a symbol of love and life. Love overcomes failure by reversing its meaning, by giving it a new meaning, a positive, redeeming meaning that becomes the message and good news of the disciples of Jesus" (*A Theology of Failure* [New York: Paulist Press, 1974], p. 3).

[19]Christians have long affirmed that God himself is eternally relational, existing from all eternity in the mysterious community of persons called the Trinity. If this is the case, it is not surprising that human beings, created by God in his own image, are made for relationships.

[20]David said, "You [God] desire truth in the inner parts" (Ps 51:6 NIV). I take that to mean, among other things, that God longs for us to be honest and truthful with him and with others from the depths of our being.

[21]For a helpful discussion of shame and the way that God deals with our shame through the cross of Christ, see Christopher J. H. Wright, *The God I Don't Understand: Reflections on Tough Questions of Faith* (Grand Rapids: Zondervan, 2008), pp. 135-41.

[22]This is the thesis of Richard Lamb's book, *The Pursuit of God in the Company of Friends* (Downers Grove, Ill.: InterVarsity Press, 2003).

[23]Bruce Demarest described four categories of spiritual helpers (ranging from the more informal, unstructured and reciprocal to the more formal, structured and one-directional): spiritual friends, spiritual guides, spiritual mentors and spiritual directors. Common to all of them are vital Christian faith; knowledge of Scripture, human persons and life; loving concern; discernment; and some experience of suffering and failure (*Satisfy Your Soul*, pp. 187-218). It is surely significant that our own experience of failure is one of the things that qualifies us to be most helpful to others.

[24]Note the connection Paul made between our being comforted by God and our being able to comfort others: "Praise be to the God and Father of our Lord Jesus Christ, the Father of compassion and the God of all comfort, who comforts us in all our troubles, so that we can comfort those in any trouble with the comfort we ourselves receive from God" (2 Cor 1:3-4).

[25]This is what Paul rejoiced in at the end of his life. "I have fought the good fight, I have finished the race, I have kept the faith" (2 Tim 4:7).

[26]John T. Dunlop, *Finishing Well to the Glory of God: Strategies from a Christian Physician* (Wheaton, Ill.: Crossway, 2011), p. 79.

[27]For the following discussion, I am indebted to Pastor Laura S. Truax and her sermon "Living the Real Messy, Real Good Story," given at LaSalle Street Church, Chicago, on November 2, 2008.

[28]When we "forget what is behind," we should not only have in mind forgetting our past failures and their all-too-often paralyzing discouragement, guilt and regret. We also need to "forget" our past successes in the sense that we not allow them to make us complacent. Finally, and continuing with the race metaphor Paul used, we need to "forget" all those things in life that would distract our focus from the finish line.

[29]Wikipedia, "Queen Victoria" <http://en.wikipedia.org/wiki/Victoria_of_the_United_Kingdom>.

[30]Walter Wangerin Jr., *Ragman and Other Cries of Faith* (San Francisco: Harper & Row, 1984), p. 89.

[31]Mark made it clear that these religious leaders knew their place in the story. After Jesus finished the parable, "the chief priests, the teachers of the law and the elders looked for a way to arrest him because they knew he had spoken the parable against them" (Mk 12:12).

[32]For example, in Luke 19:41-44, Jesus wept over Jerusalem, because its inhabitants had not recognized that God was in fact coming to save them.

[33]This agonizing cry from Jesus on the cross is a quotation from Psalm 22:1. Certainly Jesus understood this verse, and he meant for us to understand his words, in terms of the entirety of Psalm 22, which concludes with praise to the God who had been faithful to this sufferer. But in no way does this reality deny the horrific, agonizing reality of the cross in which God the Father turned his back on his only Son as he laid on him all the sins of all his people.

[34]The Jesuit theologian John Navonne interpreted the rejection of Jesus' final days as an experience of failure (*A Theology of Failure*, pp. 1-3). While this designation is helpful to capture the reality and the intensity of Jesus' sorrow and grief as he experienced his rejection, we must be clear that Jesus did not fail in any ultimate sense of the word. Certainly he did not fail in any moral or spiritual sense. And the ultimate vindication of his heavenly Father shows that God himself did not in any way view Jesus as a failure.

[35]Because the incarnate Son of God fully and completely shares our humanity, he was tempted with this human assessment of his life and his ministry as a "failure." And we dare not underestimate, in a docetic way, the depth and strength of those feelings. But Scripture assures us that, though Christ was tempted in every

way as we have been, he was completely without sin. No sin on his part caused the rejection he experienced from others. And there was no sin in the way he subjectively interpreted and experienced his rejection.

[36]Paul reflected on this same connection in his famous hymn of praise to Christ in Philippians 2. After exalting Christ, who from the beginning is "in very nature God," Paul narrated his servantlike humility and obedience and God the Father's response to it. Christ "made himself nothing by taking the very nature of a servant, being made in human likeness. And being found in appearance as a human being, he humbled himself by becoming obedience to death— even death on a cross! *Therefore* God exalted him to the highest place and gave him the name that is above every name" (Phil 2:6-9, emphasis added).

[37]Though he was without sin, Jesus is able to empathize with us even in our experience of sinful failure.

[38]The goal of following the example of Jesus is stressed throughout the New Testament. This is true of specific examples of Jesus, such as his servanthood in washing his disciples' feet ("Now that I, your Lord and Teacher, have washed your feet, you also should wash one another's feet. I have set you an example that you should do as I have done for you," Jn 13:14-15), and his suffering in faith and obedience to the will of his Father ("To this you were called, because Christ suffered for you, leaving you an example, that you should follow in his steps," 1 Pet 2:21). Other times the goal is expressed more generally, as in 1 John 2:6, "Whoever claims to live in him must live as Jesus did."

Chapter 8: Helping Others

[1]Novelist Susan Howatch used the phrase "glittering image" to denote the persona we are often tempted to project. In her very insightful novel *Glittering Images*, she traced the spiritual journey of an Anglican priest named Charles Ashworth. On assignment from his bishop, Charles finds himself in a complex and very stressful situation that pushes him until he is no longer able to sustain the glittering image he so diligently sought to project. But through the help of a wise and discerning spiritual director, Father Darrow, Charles is finally able to acknowledge the glittering image and his deep fear that without it, others will not like him or find him acceptable. This sets the stage for significant new freedom and growth for Charles (Susan Howatch, *Glittering Images* [New York: Knopf, 1987]).

[2]Crawford W. Loritts Jr., *Leadership as an Identity: The Four Traits of Those Who Wield Lasting Influence* (Chicago: Moody Press, 2009), p. 96.

[3]It may be helpful to think of the openness a pastor should express in terms of concentric circles. Every pastor should have an inner circle, consisting of one's spouse, close friends and accountability partners, with whom she or he

is very open and transparent. The next circle could involve those not in the innermost circle yet who still possess significant closeness of relationship: fellow staff members, elders, good friends. The widest circle is the congregation as a whole, who are addressed from the pulpit. The level of openness and transparency expressed in preaching should be significant and real, yet undoubtedly not at the same level as expressed in the other circles. Also, the timing of disclosure is important. Pastoral counselor Jerry Law says that for pastors who are themselves in recovery, there is an absolutely crucial need for rigorous honesty to an appropriate inner circle (a counselor, one's spouse and perhaps family, a sponsor in a recovery group, the elders or church board), but it may be wisest to adopt a course of progressive disclosure with regard to the congregation as a whole ("The Transparent Pastor," *Leadership* 30, no. 2 [Spring 2009]: 49-51).

[4]Ibid., p. 47.

[5]In the previous chapter, we considered the stirring opening words of Hebrews 12 that urge us to fix our eyes on Jesus and to run with perseverance the race that God has marked out for us (Heb 12:1-2). But the author says that we are to receive encouragement to keep running in the race from the "great cloud of witnesses" that surrounds us. This great cloud consists of all those who bear witness to us that a life of persevering faith is worth it in the end and that there is grace to help us keep on running. To be sure, these witnesses are God's people throughout history (see Heb 11). But we can all be encouragers for each other. Each of us can be a significant part of the great cloud of witnesses that encourages us all to keep on running.

[6]M. Craig Barnes, "The Most Important Thing You Do," *Leadership* 20, no. 2 (Spring 1999): 50. Barnes is currently the senior pastor of Shadyside Presbyterian Church, Pittsburgh, Pennsylvania, and Robert Meneilly Professor of Pastoral Ministry at Pittsburgh Theological Seminary. When he wrote this article, he was the pastor of the National Presbyterian Church in Washington, D.C.

[7]Ibid., p. 51.

[8]This is true with any kind of suffering, not only suffering connected with failure. One of the most significant biblical examples of the ministry of presence involves the friends of Job. When they heard of the great suffering of their friend (stemming from the loss of his property, his children and his health), they went to "sympathize with him and comfort him" (Job 2:11). When they saw him and realized how great his suffering was, they began to weep and tear their own robes. "Then they sat on the ground with [Job] for seven days and seven nights. No one said a word to him, because they saw how great his suffering was" (Job 2:13). This was their finest hour. It was only after these seven days that Job began to speak in his anguish, and these three friends felt the

need to respond and to give "answers" (Job 3–31). Things went quickly down-
hill after that.

[9]Many manuscripts render Mark 1:41 as Jesus being "filled with compassion"
(NIV; in NRSV, Jesus was "moved with pity"). Undoubtedly this was true, as
Jesus' actions would indicate. But the weight of evidence seems to favor the
translation "Jesus was indignant" (TNIV). See the discussion in William Lane,
The Gospel of Mark, New International Commentary on the New Testament
(Grand Rapids: Eerdmans, 1974), pp. 84-86.

[10]Such actions were characteristic of Jesus' attitude toward the ceremonial laws
and their rituals. W. A. Wessel said that in this action, Jesus "boldly placed love
and compassion over ritual and regulation" (*Mark*, Expositor's Bible Commentary, vol. 8 [Grand Rapids: Zondervan, 1984], p. 630).

[11]Anne Lamott, *Operating Instructions: A Journal of My Son's First Year* (New York:
Anchor, 1993), p. 137.

[12]The Fellowship is a quiet ministry that seeks to operate under the radar, believing this is necessary to minister genuinely to politicians and office holders. It
does engage in public forms of ministry, such as organizing the annual National Day of Prayer. But it usually operates in a quiet (or secretive, depending
on your perspective) way. It does not have a website and offers little public information about its mission and organization. The Fellowship has also been
called "The Family" in a recent book by Jeff Sharlet that is a very negative take
on the nature and operations of the group: *The Family: The Secret Fundamental-
ism at the Heart of American Power* (New York: HarperCollins, 2008).

[13]Manuel Roig-Franzia, "The Political Enclave that Dare Not Speak Its Name: The
Sanford and Ensign Scandals Open a Door on Previously Secretive 'C Street'
Spiritual Haven," *Washington Post*, June 26, 2009 <www.washingtonpost.com/
wp-dyn/content/article/2009/06/25/AR2009062504480.html>. See also Emily
Belz and Edward Lee Pitts, "All in the Family," *World Magazine*, August 29, 2009
<http://www.worldmag.com/articles/15778>. While Sharlet's book was pub-
lished before the Ensign and Sanford scandals, he too had a negative take on the
actions of the Fellowship and their motives in these cases. This becomes clear
in interviews Sharlet had with national media figures such as Rachel Maddow,
YouTube, "Republicans Cover Up Cheating & Crime at C Street Hideaway"
<www.youtube.com/watch?v=c3AfwQ194xU>; and Chris Matthews, YouTube,
"Inside the Family" <www.youtube.com/watch?v=n8kPcJwx79w>.

[14]The various "one another" passages found throughout the New Testament
Epistles (for example, "Now that you have purified yourselves by obeying the
truth so that you have sincere love for each other, love one another deeply,
from the heart" [1 Pet 1:22]; "Carry each other's burdens, and in this way you
will fulfill the law of Christ" [Gal 6:2]; and "Encourage one another daily, as

long as it is called 'Today,' so that none of you may be hardened by sin's deceitfulness" [Heb 3:13]) provide ample warrant for concluding that the relational help we need to thrive is not meant to come from pastors and church leaders only. We are all called to love, bear burdens, encourage, confess to and pray for one another.

[15]There is a wonderful example of this in the Old Testament. After David had been anointed by the prophet Samuel as the next king of Israel, but before he actually became king, he had to flee for his life from Saul, the current king. When he was in the desert village of Horesh, he learned that, once again, Saul had come out to take his life. But God protected David and provided him with a friend—Jonathan, Saul's son. But the help Jonathan provided for David was ultimately God-centered. We read in 1 Samuel 23:16, "And Saul's son Jonathan went to David at Horesh and helped him find strength in God." As important and needed as Jonathan's friendship and help was, David's strength was to be found in God himself. And God is the one Jonathan pointed David to. So it must be with us; we also need to point ourselves and those we serve again and again to God and to his Son, Jesus Christ.

[16]See, for example, the very helpful treatment of the crucial and indispensable relationship between social justice and worship by Mark Labberton, *The Dangerous Act of Worship: Living God's Call to Justice* (Downers Grove, Ill.: InterVarsity Press, 2007). He argues that just as faithful worship of God cannot be separated from concern for the spread of God's justice in the world, so justice-filled love for one's neighbor cannot be separated from love for God. On the latter issue, see especially chapter six, "Doing Justice Begins with Rest."

Scripture Index